Writing
After Fifty

by Leonard L. Knott

**How to find—enjoy—and make money
from a new career as a writer
AFTER you retire**

Cincinnati, Ohio

Library of Congress Cataloging in Publication Data

Knott, Leonard L.
    Writing after fifty.

    Bibliography: p.
    Includes index.
    1. Authorship. 2. Aged as authors. I. Title.
PN147.K67   1985   808'.02   85-12004
ISBN 0-89879-191-X

Design by Charleen Catt Lyon

Dedicated to my son, Leonard L. Knott, Jr., who at fifty, much to his amazement, becomes eligible for membership in the American Association of Retired Persons. In 1984, he would have been told to serve a fifteen-year "apprenticeship" in the National Association of Mature People, but the trend to early retirement changed all that. It also changed the title of this book, which began as *Writing After Sixty* and was altered in midstream to *Writing After Fifty*.

Youth, large, lusty, loving,
Youth, full of grace, force, fascination,
Do you know that Old Age may come after you
With equal grace, force, fascination?

Walt Whitman
Youth, Day, Old Age and Night

There's nothing wrong with
retirement as long as it doesn't
get in the way of my work.

B. Frowt, at 81

Contents

INTRODUCTION

In the United States and Canada today, there are more than 25 million men and women who are sixty-five or over. By the year 2000, Senior Citizens will account for more than half the eligible voters in these two countries.

People are living longer. More importantly, they are staying healthy, vigorous, and creative longer. Many of them, freed from the burden of earning a living, are seeking new ways to employ the talents they may have long neglected or never knew they had.

There are already many more opportunities open to the "late bloomers" and mature achievers than there have ever been before. The Voice of Experience is not only being heard in the land but is being heeded and encouraged. Men and women once regarded as far past their prime are serving as counselors, part-time teachers, and scientific advisers; starting new businesses, going to art schools and photography classes to find new ways of expressing bottled up emotions and ideas.

Many older people are doing *for the first time* something they've always wanted to do. They're writing books and magazine articles, newspaper features and family histories, community records and poetry. They are learning about language and literature and how difficult yet simple it is to become a writer.

Many of these people have discovered there is a market for what they write if they develop the skills they already have. The checks they receive are a welcome addition to pensions or savings.

Not everyone, at any age, can write a saleable manuscript—but neither will every Senior artist or photographer find a market for his or her pictures. All, however, may enjoy the thrill of creation and, for many, there is a reasonable prospect of a small pot of gold at the end of the rainbow.

After retirement, you probably won't have a baby, but you may learn how to create something as uniquely your own. Helping you to do that is what this book is about.

ONE

Welcome to the
Senior Writers' Club

When I was ten, I was sure I'd never measure up. When I was twenty-one, I was scared to death of life. When I was seventy, I felt life to be a breeze.

Agneta Jensen, Golden Ager; written in 1977 when she attended a poetry writing class. From *I Never Told Anybody; Teaching Poetry in a Nursing Home* by Kenneth Koch

At the half-century mark, you've already done a heap of living, but in this live-longer age you could still have a lot to look forward to.

Cross that age barrier that separates the young sheep from the old goats and you may have arrived at the best, and possibly the only, productive writing days of your life. You may even become famous, or wealthy, or beloved by your friends and neighbors, or just have fun. The horizon may be a little darker and a whale of a lot nearer than it used to be, but all the experts say that at sixty-five, the Magic Number, there's still lots of good weather ahead. You may even live long enough to see your manuscripts in print and your name in type on a book or magazine or newspaper articles. You could be the creator of your very own five-foot book shelf or a hefty mass of clippings with your name attached—living proof that you once walked this earth and captured with words some of its magic.

A "young" friend of mine who's seventy-two confessed to me recently that he would like to write his life story but felt he was too old to start a project he would probably never complete. I told him to read the epilogue in James Branch Cabell's book of recollections, particularly the paragraph in which he reminded his readers that Walter Savage Landor wrote till he was eighty-nine; George Bernard Shaw was still writing at ninety-four, and Moses ben-Amran "did not relinquish active authorship til he was 120." Using those examples, at sixty-five, you've got anywhere from twenty to fifty-five productive years as a writer left. Who could ask for more? Even the most prolific authors could say all they had to say in less than fifty years.

There are thousands, perhaps millions, of men and women in their seventies and eighties, and some in their nineties or into their second century, who are as mentally alert and creatively active as they were in their forties. Many of them are smarter than they were then, learn more rapidly, absorb new knowledge and new ideas more readily, and have a great and stimulating memory bank to boot.

Sister St. Michael Guindon, founder of the Canadian Institute of Religion and Gerontology, puts it this way: "You don't lose all your marbles the day you become sixty-five. People keep telling me you can't teach an old dog new tricks, but I tell them no one has yet told the dog and he just goes right on learning." In her eighties, Sister St. Michael goes right on writing.

MRS. WHISTLER, MEET GRANDMA MOSES

The only reason there aren't more dynamic and creative Senior Citizens around is that old age was considered unfashionable and they were conned into believing they should be neither seen nor heard, should accept retirement gracefully and withdraw not only from whatever occupations they were engaged in but also (figuratively if not literally) from the human race. Their place, they were told, was in a rocking chair or a nursing home; their sole remaining function was to fade quietly away. Retirement spelled "finish"; the only decent thing was to behave as proper old people should and wait for the day or night when they would finally expire.

Well, that's not for this Senior—or for millions of others. For us, there are still many new worlds to conquer; for many of us, one of those new worlds is the world of creative writing. There are ways to make this all come true, even for those who've never written a creative word in their lives but who often wished they had.

Not all the old-age myth makers, of course, were jealous underlings eager to get rid of the established competition. Some of them were gentle, kindhearted people—including writers and artists—who contributed to the myth by painting sympathetic and loving pictures of the elderly. Most famous, perhaps, is the painting of Whistler's *Artist's Mother*. There for all to see is a devoted son's portrait of a gracious old lady (she was all of forty-nine), lace bonnet and all, sitting quietly embroidering or sewing, a sweet, sad expression on her face, serenely awaiting her final end. She became the symbol of old age the way it ought to be. Millions have viewed Mrs. Whistler, either in the Louvre in Paris where the original painting hangs, or in reproductions in books and magazines, as calendar art, or framed pictures in living rooms, schools, and libraries around the world.

Alongside, in many an old mansion, were steel engravings of the *Angelus*, or drawings of weary grandparents with stooped shoulders being taken for walks by their sturdy grandchildren. Great art they may not be, but they expressed the sentiments of the young for the old and won worldwide acceptance for a wrong idea.

Contrast these with the spry, talented late-starter Grandma Moses, who sprang to fame as a "primitive artist" in her eighties and wrote the story of her life when she was in her nineties. Or contrast them with the mother of Anthony Trollope. Trollope reported in his *Autobiography* (still good reading for aspiring authors) that his mother wrote her first book when she was fifty, a description of her first visit to America. During the next twenty-six years, she had 113 more books published and made enough money from them to keep her family in reasonable comfort.

Then there was that early retiree, Napoleon Bonaparte, who, when he was on board HMS *Bellarophon* en route to his retirement home on St. Helena, is reported to have said: "Whatever shall we do in that remote spot? Well, we will write our memoirs. Work is the scythe of time." Well spoken, that one-time scourge of Europe.

And finally for now, hearken to a contemporary eighty-two-year-old Melville Bennett, retired British schoolteacher who in 1984 completed his first novel, *The Bloody Crown of Keltiga*. It's not likely you'll read it: It's written in Cornish, a language that only an estimated 300 people can read. "I'm not expecting to make my fortune," the former teacher said, "or become internationally famous."

SWINGING SENIORS

A Canadian psychologist, John Towler of Waterloo University, is especially critical of writers of children's books and newspaper columns who repeat the libel against their elders and even pass it along to television. Invariably, he says, everyone over sixty-five is shown as a quaint, feeble grandparent, or a toothless witch or wizard. "The message in print and television is that older people are not important." He adds hopefully, "As the number of active and creative older people grows, publishers and producers will realize they have a growing market they won't be able to afford to ignore."

When we were young, grandfathers and grandmothers generally behaved as writers and artists were wont to describe them. With few exceptions, they were content to live with their children, putter in the garden, make patchwork quilts, or crochet doilies and antimacassars to cover the exposed arms of living-room chairs and sofas. They were often accepted as unwanted boarders or "house guests" in the homes of their children, who tried to keep them out of sight or used them to babysit with their own offspring.

There may be some of that today, but I wouldn't count on it Grandpa and Grandma are more likely to be found on the golf course, out sailing or wind-surfing, or joining in cross-country marathons. You'll find them at rock concerts, whooping and stomping along with the kids, dropping in at the town's afternoon "happy hours" and living in their own houses or condominiums. Even when they finally land in a Senior Citizen's home, the lucky ones continue to live a kind of jet set life with cocktail lounges, portable bars, bingo games, and nights at the races. An astonishing number bang away at typewriters, or even click away at word processors, turning out highly readable and saleable manuscripts. The life of quiet desperation ain't what it used to be. Thank goodness!

Those who write are discovering that nostalgia is the "in" thing—or, as the president of the American Association of Retired Persons reported on her return from a trip to Paris, in the City of Light, "Age is the rage."

Many of us who are already living in this Brave New World that old-line cynics once called "Life after life" don't fully appreciate the changes which have taken place during the past few decades and which are continuing at an even more rapid pace. New opportunities and new challenges that would have daunted much younger people even a quarter of a century ago exist all around us.

A man of seventy-three who used to be a movie star was elected President of the United States with the largest majority on record. He enjoyed it so much that he's even gone back for a second stint of doing what's been described as the biggest job on earth. Willard Espy, master anagrammer, produced his thirteenth book at age seventy-three. He wrote his first when he was sixty. Espy's delight is playing with words. In his book, *The Game of Words,* he says: "I treat the words as pets, to be stroked or kicked according to their deserts, and my whim." I cite Mr. Espy here not because he is still writing at seventy-four but because he has found something new to do with words and obviously enjoys what he is doing. With Mr. Espy, as well as with Mr. President, the key word is *enjoy*—a fine one for those over fifty looking to the future.

This new retirement-time attitude is partly, perhaps mainly, a result of the Baby Boom in the forties and fifties. The little codgers we complained about as we dug in our pockets to find the cash to build more and more schools, playgrounds, and child care centers are close to becoming old codgers now, and they're not inclined to give up the good life they've enjoyed. They are already influencing our old age mores, and those under fifty are beginning to see us an an economic asset instead of a drag.

INFLUENTIAL SENIORS

Business and financial communities, as well as the arts and leisure world, are noticing our presence. We're in the market for more than crutches and bifocal contact lenses. Our disposable income (to use a cliché favored by economists and financial writers who shun the simple word "cash") outranks that of the teenagers who were the darlings of the marketeers in the sixties and seventies. And we have time to indulge our interests: Nothing drags us away from our interest in spending. Everything from cosmetics to motor cars is being designed for the elderly, who are becoming increasingly numerous, healthy, and long-lived, with a proportional rise in buying power both as a group and as individuals.

Evidence of this commercial recognition of the gerontological revolution is plain to read. Department stores run weekly Seniors' Days—commonly a 10 percent discount on all the store's merchandise and free coffee with lunch. Transportation companies give discounts, and theaters promote Golden Age clubs. Much more important is the trend in the communications industry. Books and magazines of the future will reflect this change and are already carrying more items of special interest to Senior readers. Many radio and television programs are being slanted to "mature audiences" and, trust me, mature today doesn't mean twenty-one—it means fifty-plus.

A case in point: In Washington, D.C., radio station WJAY-AM/FM caters to a large mature audience. In 1984, the station had lots of listeners but a paucity of advertisers. Companies with the spending cash needed to keep WJAY on the air were still running hard after young rock and rollers.

Station manager Ted Dorf sensed they were out of date. "Everywhere you go these days you read and hear of the 'graying of America,' how people are living longer, have healthier lifestyles. They're the new growth market of the eighties," he said. A group of mature station managers, station reps, and program directors was formed to give the advertisers the message. The first thing the group did was put the old age community under a microscope, figuratively speaking, and bring out facts to convince those who said there was no future in selling to a market that kept losing its constituents.

A lively interest in the Seniors market appeared when it was shown that by the year 2000 it will have jumped from 47 million people over fifty to 58.7 million, whereas the juvenile and adult population below fifty-five will have declined. The Seniors market will rank high in demand for travel services, cars, appliances, and hobby materials. Attention, Madison Avenue: The old age boom is just about upon us.

WRITING IS GOOD FOR YOU

Medical doctors generally approve of the newly generated creative activity among their older patients and consider it good therapy. (The exception is my personal physician who, every time my wife visits his office, asks her why I keep up this insane activity running about from town to town, radio station to radio station, and staying up all hours typing. She doesn't have the answer and probably thinks I'm crazy too.) Popularly expressed medical opinion, however, is that physical activity is necessary to good health, and mental activity, involving as it does a continuing interest in living, is even more beneficial than jumping up and down on a gym floor or walking a mile after breakfast. Interested (and interesting) people live longer.

Writing is, or should be, a lively intellectual activity for anyone, even the physically handicapped, with imagination, curiosity, and initiative. It offers a healthy and profitable old-age occupation—possibly even a new and exciting career.

MAKING NEW CONTACTS
The real problem in old age, according to eighty-year-old Dr. B. F. Skinner, Harvard psychologist, is one that particularly concerns those who write. It is not so much how to have ideas as how to use them. And for this, maintenance of contacts outside the old age world is important.

Maintaining old contacts for any length of time is a rare luxury for aging citizens, and developing new ones is not that much easier. If, during our active years, we worked outside the home, our friends and acquaintances are most likely to be found among our business associates. Bus drivers meet other bus drivers; office managers meet fellow executives and middle ranking employees; skilled workers fraternize with other trades and craft workers on the factory floor. These "contacts" for the most part disappear when we go "over the hill" to that never-never land where nobody works anymore!

When I retired after forty-five years in the newspaper and public relations business, I remembered my last few years when former associates whom I had once found my most fascinating companions would drop in on my office once in a while "just to say hello" and ask how things were going. The first few times, I was glad to see them and talk old times. But then they always seemed to stay too long; they were out of touch with what I was doing and had nothing of interest to tell me about their new vocation: growing old. I instructed my secretary to tell them I was busy or out. Their visits ended. I was no longer a "contact" for them.

Women who worked in the home were better off. Their contacts were made with neighbors, church members, clubs and social organizations. Still, they suffered from some of the same problems affecting their spouses. As they aged, their contacts moved to other communities, to warmer climates, to locales near their children, to Senior Citizen apartments, rest homes, and convalescent hospitals.

As we "graduate" from old contact networks, we must find ways to make new ones. Those of us who take up writing as a new or part-time career have a big advantage. Writing means meeting people, gathering information, going places, and having new experiences. These provide new opportunities for making friends, developing common interests with those we interview, and building a new and often much younger range of intellectual companionship.

In most communities there are numerous clubs and study groups. Join those that share your interests. If you are a popular science fan and are fascinated by the stars, join an astronomy club or take a course at your local university or community college. If it's history that interests you, mingle with the local historical society. Best of all, if you're serious about writing, go back to school. Register for English 101, or a creative writing course; sign up for lectures or demonstrations on computers and word processors. Whatever you study, you'll find fellow students your own age, younger, or even (you've got to believe it) much older. They'll be your new contacts, your fresh network.

And if you want extra companionship, you can try visiting Senior Citizen Centers which, thanks to government grants and charitable donations, now exist in almost every community. There you'll find bingo players, bridge and even checkers addicts, and a multitude of crafters—men and women who make birdhouses, potholders and intricate patchwork quilts, and varieties of dolls and stuffed animals. They're busy, they're creative, and if you can share their interests, you've got the makings of new contacts. And although you may want to keep one foot firmly planted in the middle-age world which rightly regards you as a Senior, unless you're Methuselah, you're always going to be Junior to somebody. It can be good to remind yourself of that every now and again.

THE EIGHTIES—AND BEYOND

There are many examples of successful writers and artists who continued their creative activities long past retirement age and in many cases did their best work when they were in their seventies and eighties. Picasso painted furiously until his death at ninety-two. In 1983, Morley Callaghan, the Canadian novelist who knocked out Hemingway in a boxing bout in Paris, published his twentieth novel and took off on a media tour across the continent to publicize it. He was only eighty and already talking of his next book. A more prolific, though younger, example is Louis l'Amour, the world's record Western writer. Well into his seventies, he published his eighty-fourth book in 1983 and saw his all-time book sales go over the 130 million mark. He showed no signs of slowing down and was busy on book number eighty-five.

There are fewer examples of well-known writers, men or women, who *began* their writing careers after sixty-five, although Helen Hooven Santmyer, author of . . . *And Ladies of the Club*, (about whom I have more to say later) comes quickly to mind. Still, there are many who did their first writing after retirement and have been published and paid for their work. (OK, their payment was often a pittance, but it helps pay the grocery bills.) And there'll be many more Senior Citizen beginners as the word gets around that it's never too late to learn.

Of the well-known new post-retirement authors, most are men and women who had fascinating careers in politics, business, theater, or the arts. If we wonder sometimes at their writing skill, there may be a ghost writer back there somewhere, but many do write their own stories, some of them remarkably well.

Charles Ritchie, Canadian ambassador to Washington during the Kennedy and Johnson administrations, is a retired diplomat whose delightfully written memoirs make one regret he did not forsake diplomacy for literature much earlier. But maybe that would have been a mistake. As a Senior Citizen beginner, he drew on a lifetime rich with experiences and conversations with the high and the mighty. They undoubtedly enriched his vocabulary and contributed to his style—a style which, by the way, he developed through constant writing in a carefully composed diary.

English literature would have been the poorer, and many important historical facts and interpretations would never have been known had it not been for people in high places who never thought of becoming professional writers but who confided in their diaries. When their time came to retire and they had leisure time to go back over their records, they discovered that the transition from diary keeping to writing for publication was simplified. They had, as it were, twenty or thirty years of examining, reporting, and exposing on paper matters both trivial and important—a continuing course in creative writing.

"ORDINARY PEOPLE"

But what about the common folk, the "ordinary" men and women who have not lived romantic or adventurous lives and have no recollections of meeting with suave and polished international figures to draw on? No wonderful anecdotes about the rich and famous to be found in their diaries (if indeed they ever kept diaries)? More likely are references to a family dinner party, paying off the mortgage on the house, or a trip to the state capital. Trivial and unimportant entries they may seem, but they are the stuff of which thousands of books are made. And recording them carefully and thoughtfully may help you, like Charles Ritchie, develop a style that will make some future manuscript a joy to read. As well, your diary notes may serve as a practical memory jogger to boost not only your later writing career but help you win arguments with your spouse and other forgetful friends and relatives. Ideally, diaries should begin as soon as you have something memorable to record—such as being born. But, whatever your age, your diary can begin today and be your companion through life. Like ripening cheese, it will improve with age.

Seemingly ordinary people can, late in life, become extraordinary writers. Consider, for instance, Laura E. Crews, who lived on a farm till she was eighty-five, when she broke her hip. Confined to a wheelchair, she turned to writing books and articles. Five of her published books were still in print in 1982 and she was working on a sixth. Her titles included: *My Kinsfolk, Original Poems by Us Kinfolk, Tell Me A Story,* and *Reminiscences of Us Kinsfolk.* Not even a teeny item about a prince or princess or a foreign diplomat in the lot. Interviewed by Osborn Segerberg, Jr., for his book *Living to be 100,* Miss Crews, by then a centenarian, said, "It's always my theory that allowing your mind to become inactive causes senility."

Henriette S. Dull, another American who lived beyond the 100-year mark, published her first book, *Southern Cookbook,* in 1928, when she was sixty-five. It's still in print and regarded in the South as the bible of Confederate cuisine. Grandma Moses, whom I mentioned earlier, was discovered as a painter when she was in her eighties. Yet before she died, she wrote her first book, *My Life History,* outlining all her attitudes toward life—a work that should be better known.

And finally, Segerberg's cast of centenarians includes one Joseph A. de Muth, of Glendale, California. De Muth started to write poetry when he was in his nineties and composed a long poem in celebration of his hundredth birthday. One stanza was as follows:

> *While talking with a doctor*
> *About accidents and ills,*
> *He said I have lived longer 'cause*
> *I tossed aside his pills.*

Not a candidate for a Pulitzer, perhaps, but it sounded pretty good to de Muth's family when he read it out, all ten or more stanzas, at his birthday party.

Critics and, more importantly, readers are discovering there's something particularly appealing about the writings of old men and women who have lived interesting but unpublicized lives. Their years, after all, were not always filled with uninspiring toil. They lived, they laughed, they sinned, and they wept. They had successes and failures. And of such human experiences all literature, great or ordinary, is composed.

NEVER TOO BUSY, NEVER TOO LATE

It's often been said that within every man and woman there is at least one story. In fact, within most people there are a dozen or more stories. People we all know have expressed a desire to tell their story or stories in prose or poetry, in a book or in a song, or simply in a homemade journal or in letters. For most of their lives, this desire remains unfulfilled, the stories inside fade, still untold. Not because the stories refuse to come out, but because their owners are too busy—raising a family (or raising hell), earning a living, discovering the world, or playing games.

"I know I could write if I only had the time," is the oft-heard complaint. "I was always good in composition at school and once I had a novel half-finished. Then I was sent off to another job (or another baby came) and I got so busy I forgot all about it. The manuscript is still around, tucked in a drawer someplace. I'd love to write, but I simply don't have the time. 'Tisn't that I couldn't do it."

Too busy to write! No one could have been busier than Teresa Bloomingdale, who found time between running a house and raising ten children to write four popular books: *I Should Have Seen It Coming When the Rabbit Died*, *Up a Family Tree*, *Murphy Must Have Been a Mother*, and *Life Is What Happens When You're Making Other Plans*, all published by Doubleday. And who says Jean Kerr, wife of the *New York Times* drama critic, wasn't well occupied as the mother of five sons and a daughter? Yet somehow she found the time to write *Please Don't Eat the Daisies*, *The Snake Has All the Lines*, and *How I Got to Be Perfect*, also from Doubleday, and several plays that were produced on Broadway.

What on earth are these two ladies going to do when they retire? Switch to engineering? Or be rocking chair grandmothers?

This too-busy-to-write complex applies even to many people who are already in the professional writing business; the field is full of newspaper reporters who are always at work on their half-finished and never-completed novel, librarians who have half a dozen unfinished poems in with the filing cards somewhere, and news columnists who are always on the verge of writing their book of exposés. Oh, if they only had the time!

On a recent media tour when I was being interviewed by the newspaper, radio, and television reporters and commentators, eight of the first nine interviewers confessed they had half finished or barely started fiction stories at home. "I've got the greatest idea for a short story since the invention of printing," one of them told me. "I got the idea when I was a junior in radio, just out of college. I've started writing it several times but then I just got too busy. Funny thing is when I look at it now, I have a completely different idea of how it should turn out. Someday, I'm going to finish it—but whoops, hold on, we're on the air. . . ."

Why not finish it later? He's started adding experience to ideas. He's met new people and that's changed some of his characterizations. When he retires and gets back to his "inside story," just don't let anyone tell him it's too late. At least, he'll have something more to say than when he was a callow youth of forty or so.

A woman TV interviewer told me she gets marvelous ideas for her unfinished novel from interviewing her guests. "I just don't have the time to write them," she said. "TV is a very demanding boss; it eats up copy, and people, like a dog eats kibbles."

"Make notes about all those interesting people in your journal," I suggested, "and keep adding to them till you retire. Then, when you get back to writing, you'll have a bookful of your own special characters to draw from."

"Till I retire," she laughed. "I'm only thirty. I can't wait that long, but right now I just don't have the time."

Don't worry, dear. You never will have the time till you retire, and retirement, I'm sorry to say, will come much sooner than you think. You're halfway there already, and by the time you're fifty, that may have become the compulsory cut-off date.

Twenty, thirty, forty years later, these no-time writers will have all the time they need. They'll be retired, perhaps unwillingly, and they'll grumble about being put out to pasture, often just to make way for some bright kid. Their children will have left the family nest and gone off to raise kids and enmesh themselves in their own time-consuming jobs. What's left? Time—what retirees have in common. They may spend the first few weeks or months wondering what to do with it.

If they really did want to write, and particularly if they were smart enough to keep some kind of diary or journal or other form of memory jogger, they need wonder no longer. Now they can get at those stories they've harbored all these many years. They can find out if they really are poets or novelists or short story writers and if they have anything interesting to say.

WRITERS ARE THE MOST MOBILE OF ARTISTS —EVEN IN WHEELCHAIRS

Once the no-timers have retired, the opportunity they always begged for is at hand. They can write for fun (and there's not a thing wrong with that) or they can write for money; if they don't need to be concerned about the money, they can combine the two. Either way, writing is the one post-retirement activity that doesn't require a great change in your way of life. It's something you can do in your own home, in a country cabin beside the lake while the spouse splashes about with energetic grandchildren (if you have any), or up in the attic or in a basement family room.

To go back to Anthony Trollope for a moment: in addition to being a popular novelist, Mr. Trollope was a high official of the British post office. In the process of setting up rural mail routes in England in the mid-1800s, he had to travel all over the country. "I found that I passed in railway carriages very many hours of my existence," he wrote in his autobiography. "I made for myself a little tablet and I found I could write as quickly in a railway carriage as I could at my desk." That shows that wherever there's enough light, dry paper, and a pen, a writer can write.

You may take your writing on an overseas trip, on a bus or a boat. With today's electronic equipment, you don't even have to haul heavy typewriters about or worry about running out of paper: You can just sling your miniature tape recorder around your neck. If you get the kind with earphones, you can speak-write your story on the move and let someone else (your husband or wife, perhaps, or a newfound Senior playmate) do the typing. Or you may simply leave it there on tape for "talking book" readers to enjoy. Such is the peculiarity of the English language, that it is now quite proper to refer to speaking into a microphone as "writing," and our libraries are filled with books that talk out loud. If that's your method, though, be careful you don't push the wrong button and inadvertently erase part of your story, thus performing a function usually reserved for some disgruntled editor.

With equal ease, if the second stage of your long retirement

means you're hoisted out of your comfortable home and con-
signed to Senior Citizens' quarters or a nursing home, you can
drag your typewriter or tape recorder and all your ideas and fantasies along with you, and keep right at it. You may wobble a bit
when you walk or have to move about in a wheelchair, but up top
your think box is as good as ever *if you keep it working.* You may
sympathize with the retired artist whose work was with heavy
stone or marble, or the cabinetmaker who needs a twenty-foot
lathe. But you'll have what *you* need to be creative.

There have been instances of popular writing coming out of
"last stop" residences where nobody was supposed to have anything to say: products of humanity's indomitable spirit and the
determination of some aging person determined to learn how to
write.

An eighty-year-old bird watcher friend of mine writes her
stories on the bus on her way from a day's watching among the
warblers. Stuart Richardson, a Senior Citizen's retirement home
resident, thinks poetry as he waits his turn on the bowling green.
Of course, he's only eighty-five and has been writing verse, whenever he had the time, for fifty years.

All this writing in strange places is not just wasted energy or
playing at being active and trying to pretend one is still part of a
busy, busy world. If one goes at it intelligently, and surely that's
something we should have learned in our regulated Junior years,
there's a market for our talents. All the market needs is a little extra cultivating and some serious effort at finding one's way in.
Ours could be one of the 50,000 books to be published in the United States or Canada this year.

If and when you move to smaller premises, into a Seniors'
residence or nursing home, don't throw away those notes and
journals you've kept all this while. Hang onto the fantasies that
obsessed you when you were fifty and never had time to get into
print. You might one day see some of those hastily scrawled sentences turn to gold.

If you don't believe me but are willing to be convinced, stay
aboard for the next few chapters and I'll introduce you to the
Wonderful World of Golden Age Writers, a world which never really existed till now and is part of society's new approach to aging.
I'll show you, too, how to enjoy and earn a few dollars by exercis-

ing a talent you always knew you had but never did anything about. I won't promise you roses: The likelihood of your writing a best seller and reaping a harvest of dollars is slight, to say the least. But when you were in your prime, it's possible you weren't one of the best-dressed, highest paid people on the block. And you managed just the same, didn't you?

For the business or professional man or woman, Dale Carnegie said it a long time ago: "Life begins at forty." It was a revolutionary thought for youth-oriented America where a thirty-year-old thought that if he hadn't made his mark by then, he might just as well pack up and sneak away. But what great news it was for us who had just passed our fourth or fifth decade! No longer did we need to pretend we were thirty-nine if we aspired to the executive suite.

And today, now that we're older and wiser, we know that life can begin at fifty or sixty or even later, whenever there's something important or just plain amusing we'd like to do.

And so, for people who like to write, who have the human urge to tell a story or communicate an idea but never had time to put pen to paper, your time has come. It begins the day you sit down seriously at desk or table and say, "Now, at last, I'm going to be a writer. There's nothing to stand in my way. Let's see: Where do I begin?" The years ahead may, indeed, be your Golden Age.

No more fears, no need to be shy, no overbearing Seniors to tell you you're stupid, bombastic, vain, or vulgar because they don't like what you write. You're in the driver's seat now. At seventy, when you've matured a little more, you may find, as Agneta Jensen did, that "life is a breeze." You can write as you please . . . and you may even get published.

So here goes. Welcome to the Club.

TWO

Before You Retire,
Be a Writer in Waiting

Then all of us prepared to rise
And hold our bibs before our eyes
And be prepared for some surprise
When Father carves the duck.

Ernest Vincent Wright
"When Father Carves the Duck"
(1891)

Life, one learns after more than seven decades at it, is full of little surprises. A big one is due the day we cross over from Junior to Senior Citizen and find ourselves as hale and hearty as ever and just rarin' to go. We're about to collect a real-life bonus—ten, twenty, maybe thirty or forty years to get at those short stories, poems, essays, how-tos or that Great American Novel the whole world is waiting for us to write.

As George Burns said at his eightieth birthday celebration, "I just hope the second half of my life is as exciting as the first." We helped it to be just that for us if we started preparing for it when we were young.

This chapter is written primarily to help the next generations pave the way more efficiently for a future in which writing may provide a new full- or part-time career or just a very rewarding hobby. It may provide some useful guidelines for those who have yet to scale the heights and enter into the Golden Age. It's all about thinking and planning for the future. As John Galsworthy, who himself was no chicken, observed in one book of his *Forsyte Saga (Swan Song):* "If you do not think about the future, you cannot have one." Not literally true, perhaps, because there have been many late-blooming writers who never gave a thought to becoming scribes in their "declining" years. But it's a pertinent message for the young at any age, assuring them they'll be better off on a writing career at sixty or seventy if they've done some preparatory work along the way. They may be "too busy to write" just now, but they should never be too busy to get ready to write when their long days' labors in the vineyards are over.

WHAT'S SAUCE FOR THE GOOSE . .

There's a message here, too, for Seniors—those fifty and over—although it may appear to have come too late. Traditionally, one of the virtues (or vices) of old age has been an ability and eagerness to hand on advice to those following. Seniors can help their Juniors by giving them tips on how to prepare for their futures as writers. We may also gain some personal benefits by adapting some of what is preached here to improving our own writing habits, applying some of the tactics prescribed for the young.

Like children gathered around Ernest Wright's parental table, young and middle-aged men and women should be prepared for some surprises when they finally achieve seniority. The new world they are now entering is aglow with interesting people, exciting and invigorating and as open to new ideas, new styles, and *new writers* as the one they just left. It may even hold new challenges and opportunities for self-expression. Somewhere along the line, after one gets over the shock of being addressed as Sir or Madam and being offered a 10 percent discount on a bus ticket, there's going to be time and energy needed for the production of those long-neglected manuscripts. When that time comes, fortunate indeed will be those who have prepared for a highly creative future.

Pre-retirement training, or preparing for the final stretch, is by no means restricted to those who yearn to express themselves in print. Modern computers that reduce the number of workers required to keep Society's wheels turning, and the entry of large numbers of highly skilled women into the work force have succeeded, for the time being at least, in simultaneously reducing the number of jobs and increasing the number of bodies to fill them. The result is widespread unemployment. One probable cure will be early retirement, and that means more and more Seniors looking for something to do.

Even those who are now in their twenties and thirties are being conditioned for that future shock. My twenty-four-year-old grandson, a Business Administration major, is already studying pension plans and travel folders. The two, he thinks, go together. One time, only death and taxes were considered inevitable; today, add early retirement and half a lifetime of reclaimed time.

Universities and colleges, governments, industrial, commercial and professional employers, and labor unions are racing to anticipate the problems that will arise due to computerization and automation. They are working overtime training adult workers for life in a strange new world with diminishing demand for non-technical skills.

I was suitably amazed recently when I saw and heard the president of the National Hockey League tell an interviewer on TV that the League's most pressing problem was what to do about soon-to-be-retired hockey players. These youngsters of thirty-three and thirty-five were physically fit except for a few broken bones, but had no demonstratable skills other than putting a puck in the net. They differed from professional football players who are almost all university grads and presumably have other than athletic skills to offer a future employer. Hockey players move right into the big leagues from junior teams and high schools. The League is now planning an extensive pre-retirement educational program.

One player who didn't wait for League action was goal keeper Ken Dryden. He not only managed to acquire a law degree but upon his "retirement" became one of those rare creatures who produce a post-retirement book that becomes an instant best seller. One hesitates to refer to Ken Dryden at forty as a Senior Citizen, but he qualifies both as a retiree and as a first-time post-retirement author.

TOWARD A LIVELY OLD AGE

It's all part of our new way of life—going to pre-school to prepare for kindergarten, learning computers in kindergarten to prepare for "real" school, enrolling in "prep" schools or junior colleges to qualify for university. The Chinese and the Japanese do it better because they've been doing it longer: They simply accept the fact that all their lives are preparation for a wise, respected, and honored old age. Once there, far from being brushed aside by hot-headed youth, they're regarded as the fount of all wisdom. It would be a brave junior editor who would send a rejection slip to a Japanese author in his eighties or nineties.

Here, editors and publishers are less inclined to be influenced by the birth dates of their contributors. A 100-year-old pensioner might merit an extra look at his manuscript if it were reasonably well written and dealt with a nostalgic or historical topic involving the author personally. Also, if the writer were a well-known, famous, or even notorious personality, or someone who had enjoyed a remarkable career, a publisher might well be willing to pay well for publishing rights without even seeing the manuscript. But as for you or me, if we're fifteen or fifty the editor couldn't care less. Our submissions will be judged only by their style, content, and marketability regardless of our age, sex, or physical condition. Senior writers, in other words, will not be discriminated against. That's the good news. The bad news is that they won't be favored either. They'll face the same painful culling as the writer starting out at twenty or thirty, and believe me, that can be horrendous. Give the back of your hand to those who tell you no agent will handle your writing and no editor will publish you because you're over-age and have no long-term future. As a writer, you'll have exactly the same chance in the writers' market as your bright twenty-year-old grandchild.

During the first half of the century, men or women who changed jobs and hopped about from one profession or trade to another were considered unreliable and seldom eligible for advancement. Today, all that's changed. It's quite common for a person to have two or more careers during his working life and then go on to still another one after retirement. Yesterday's skills are becoming more and more obsolete and, to stay abreast of the constantly changing demands in the job market, one must accept the need for flexibility throughout life. Those who can do that will have no difficulty accepting the fact that beginning a writing career after fifty is no more difficult than changing careers in one's thirties or forties.

Right now in this country, if you're in your middle years, you're part of the struggle to survive, to find your way to the top of the mountain. You've a full-time job to do; you're creating a home or a business or mastering a trade or a craft. Very wisely, you consider writing a highly uncertain way of making a living. You don't have the time to do it seriously as a hobby or part-time occupation. And yet your head is buzzing with ideas.

Tim Pawsey, who lives in Vancouver, has a strong yen to write but the necessity to earn a living. He's found his own solution in a very practical way. He takes whatever writing assignments he can get and operates a floor-sanding business for his bread, butter, and rent. As he explains it: "My little floor-sanding business (Mr. Sandman, Inc.) is coming along quite nicely, and I find that aside from providing a semblance of an income it offers a pleasing balance to mind work. . . . I hope to be able to divide my time equally between that little enterprise and my writing." Meanwhile, Tim acts as summer-replacement editor for a local hotel magazine and his by-line appears on little snippets of this and that in local publications. In the works is a more grandiose project—a book on Vancouver Islands which, if necessary, he will self-publish.

Not all young people are prepared to go that far. Still, there are many ways they can prepare for the Great Day when they're unencumbered by the pressing need to work for a living. Bolstered by a pension and interest on life savings, they can take to pen or typewriter and let the literary juices flow. Imagine for a moment you are one of them.

KEEPING UP WITH THE JONESES
Last night, you were at a party at the Jones's house next door. Their uncle from Australia was there (a real rogue if you ever saw one) and he kept the room rocking with stories of adventures "down under." Lies, probably, all of them, but isn't that what stories are? Anyway, you came home muttering, "What a character!"

Hey, what's that? "What a character," you said. You could write a book about him, if you only had the time.

So you toss the idea aside with all the other story ideas you've had over the past ten years. The only one you've got on paper is the one you wrote when you were ten. It was a story about your pet canary Randolph. Your mother thought she'd given birth to a genius. She read your "book" to all your relatives and neighbors who would stop to listen. She wrapped it in tissue paper and put it in her jewel box with the label "Little Harry's First Story." You had time to write then, so you'd finished it. The stories you think of now are not treated so well. Someday, you think, you'll pick up their themes and finish them. You won't, of course, because you'll have lost the feel for them, forgotten the details, and lost interest in what they were about.

Or, you can make your visit to the Jones's worthwhile. You can begin planning to be a writer now and pin that one down. Give the sometime-in-the-future-writer (you) a break and let him have something concrete to work on.

Professional writers know that part of being an author is being a hunter—a killer, sometimes—always stalking "game," always on the alert, tracking down new characters, new ideas, following new and devious trails. It involves studying the quarry and then setting traps. You're lucky. You've just been handed a character and a whole set of little stories and plots and people and places on a platter. Make sure you don't lose them.

Write down everything you can remember—not tomorrow, not next week, but *now*. Describe the visiting uncle as you saw him. Quote his stories in his own accented speech. Get it all there, in an exercise book, a journal, a diary, or on a pad of paper. Just get it down while it's fresh in your mind. Transfer it to a more permanent and better organized journal or notebook later, perhaps. Be careful: Many well-intentioned writers who make notes at the time (I'm one of them) find that a week later, they can't read what they wrote. We scribble, trying to make our fingers keep up with our lively brain. We short-cut and abbreviate and reduce sentences by half and think we'll remember enough to translate later. We probably won't, and our efforts will be just one more labor lost.

At one time, when I was a fledgling reporter and a young man called Ernest Hemingway was a fellow newsman just a desk or two away (I didn't know how close I was to fame nor have enough sense to jot down in *my* journal words that might flow from his mouth), I invented my own brand of shorthand so I could take down court proceedings, speeches, and interviews with something resembling the speed of light. It was a great idea except that just a few hours later, when I needed them, I couldn't read my own notes.

If you plan to lay up literary treasures today to use in your retirement heaven, do it in clean, *legible* handwriting. If you can type them, so much the better. The most valuable possession a beginning Senior writer can be blessed with is a head—or better, a notebook—full of ideas, descriptions, conversations, and personal experiences.

Jerome Weidman, who likes writing funny stories about writers, says in his novel *Sound of Bow Bells:* "Writers never lived in the present. What counted was the past where the bits and pieces and lumps sucked up lay aging peacefully, like wine, against the day when they would be needed." He compared a writer to a vacuum cleaner, inhaling plots and people and situations, all to form part of some future writing. Unlike Galsworthy, who emphasized the future, Weidman stressed importance of the past. For you, as a beginning-after-retirement writer, the past is now. "Snippets of nostalgia, like scraps of pie crust, are too good to throw away," writer Connie Emerson says.

Our bits and pieces will lie there and develop most fruitfully if they are confined to a notebook, or notebooks, rather than carried about willy-nilly in our heads. Human memories are sometimes (I'd go farther and say almost always) faulty, even at the best of times. And the years over sixty-five are not considered the best of times for remembering names, dates, or conversations. Senior Citizens' memories are overcrowded and they may need some material crutches to lean on.

When we're young, or middle-aged, we may forget an appointment, fail to remember someone's name, our spouse's birthday or, God forbid, our ZIP Code. What would make us think that twenty or thirty years later, after jamming another million or so odd items about thousands of subjects into our brains, we'll remember all the details of a neighbor's conversation or our first visit to the opera? Yet those may be just the memories we'd need when we start to complete those stories or articles we'd been kicking around for years.

OUR SELECTIVE MEMORIES

We'll have some hazy ideas, of course, but they'll probably be wrong and most often influenced by prejudices or desires encountered on our way to "maturity." It's a curious fact, Schopenhauer wrote in his *Studies in Pessimism*, "that in bad days we can very vividly recall the good time that is now no more; but that in good days we have only a very cold and imperfect memory of the bad." We who are old are constantly, to the annoyance of younger companions, talking about "the good old days," forgetting that many of them were very, very bad.

If I sit down today to write something about Depression times in the thirties, I have a hard time trying to remember the bad things but easily recall all the funny things that happened—like going to parties where four of us would split a single pint of beer. I long ago forgot the despair that gripped me when I pawned my wife's engagement ring to get the money to pay the rent and keep the bailiff away from the door. But I remember very clearly the evening when I borrowed tails and a collapsible "opera hat" to travel by streetcar to a dance in a posh hotel where the price of admission was all of two dollars.

If we're looking forward to being credible as well as readable and entertaining writers, and if we want people to be seriously interested in what we write, we need more than just a few hazy ideas dragged out of far-from-perfect memory boxes cluttered with unrelated sounds, sights, smells, personal prejudices, loves, hates, and fears. Once we get into print, there'll be dozens if not hundreds of self-appointed critics waiting to pounce on every statement we make. When we put it in writing, we'd better be sure.

The time to put our memories in order is when we are creating them. They're going to be our stock-in-trade when we begin writing. That means more than just scooping up information right and left, setting it down in an assortment of higgledy-piggledy scribbled notes we won't be able to read. It might even mean we should consider keeping a diary.

"My God!" you say. "Do people still do that?" Yes, Virginia, they do, even in this sophisticated, high tech age. Many people keep diaries—particularly writing people. It may be the most arduous form of note keeping; it also has a peculiar fascination of its own and for some writers and would-be-writers it is the most effective form of self-discipline. The printed dates on ruled-off pages become cruel taskmasters.

"DEAR DIARY. . ."

Some people may find it difficult to refrain from including hints of their own brilliance in their revelations to their diaries. These intimate collections of daily activity reports also include inconsequential items needed to fill up the daily allotted space. The "inconsequential" entries may later prove even more revealing than the ponderous reporting of "important" facts. A diary may be a chore for the keeper; what a delight it may become when it's unearthed by a future author in search of a character or plot!

Diaries often become books in themselves, edited to remove obvious indiscretions or scurrilous references to those who were considered friends. The best diaries have become best sellers, and even rather mediocre ones have come to be treasure chests for social scientists, historians, and fiction writers. Where else but in a carefully guarded diary, for instance, could we find an accurate description of what President Franklin Delano Roosevelt thought of General Charles de Gaulle or what went on behind closed doors during an embassy party in Washington? On a tape, you might reply, thinking of another President's disastrous experiment with keeping on-the-spot records.

Diaries can form a solid background for articles you may one day wish to write for scholarly magazines, books of reminiscences, or Op-Ed pages in a newspaper. They may save us visits to libraries or newspaper "morgues" in search of past information of which we have only vague recollections. I know of one instance where a woman writer in her fifties was able to dig into a long-forgotten diary and come up with the lead for a history of a local institution: "Friday, January 17th, 1945 was bitterly cold. Cold enough to dampen the enthusiasm at the final performances of the Drama Festival but not enough to halt the celebrations outside the Memorial Hospital as it opened its doors for the first time." She had happened to be at both events and noted them in her diary.

We can never be sure what diary entry may eventually prove useful, but if we really think of our daily entries as aids to future writing careers, we should confine those entries to "memos" related to subjects or themes about which we think we will some day want to write. They could be about international politics, dog catching or quilt making. It might be a novel about the Mad Quilt

Maker, a humorous short story about a dogcatcher's adventures while trapping a Great Dane and finding himself frustrated by the interfering antics of a poodle, or a series of serious articles about political trends. As they say in French: *"Chacun son goût!"*

Let's say we decide on a quilting story as our first entry into the Senior Citizens' Literary Competition. Our diary could be very helpful if it had entries like this:

> Sunday, October 9, 1932: Madge and I spent weekend in Koko County, which calls itself Quilting Capital of the World. Not much of a community for a world capital but signs of active quilting everywhere. Two streets of small, neat clapboard buildings, some with gaudy quilt designs painted on outside walls . . . two quilters at work in shed of one house—one a bewhiskered man in overalls with what looked like a Civil War cap on his head—a woman about twenty—could have been his wife, busy at an easel painting quilt designs, listening to country music on a radio (Her name Dorothy Scrubble—his something like Hmmm Hmmm which is all I could hear him say; see notes later on interview) Visited home of Maggie Oppenheim (large, colonial-type mansion on outskirts of village; obviously showplace for curious visitors) . . . she's lived there sixty-two years, her parents and grandparents before her. Tiny woman, leathery complexion, hair in strings like it's never combed but sparkling, bright gray eyes that look one up and down all the time she's talking. A shrewd one for sure. Holds two world records: fastest quilter; four quilts in five days; best quilter; three gold medals and she gets as much as $1,200 each. Worked steadily while we talked; paused to pull an apple pie out of oven. Insisted we have a piece. May be great quilter but lousy cook; apples half raw, no sugar, crust like rock—smelled like burned leather. Explanation of how to make a great quilt (farther on) learned from her grandmother, a Scandinavian. Only other "hobby" pitching horseshoes. Told me she'd love to pitch one at her neighbor who keeps pinching her patterns. A nasty

Methodist she said she was; Lutherans wouldn't do a thing like that.

That's a beginning. As my editor keeps saying to me in margin notes on my manuscript: MORE—MORE—MORE.

ANOTHER "JOGGER"—THE JOURNAL

Not everyone can be a diary keeper, however. Nor is a diary by any means regarded by many writers as the best memory jogger. Many begin them, but few persevere. (Just look at the fulsome entries that occupy every date space in January, and the vast empty spaces that occupy August and September.) Many professional writers prefer to keep a journal, which may be just a sleazy schoolday exercise book or a handsome hard-cover loose-leaf binder.

A loose-leaf journal lends itself to good work organization. All the space needed for special subjects is available in separate sections that may be expanded or contracted at will. We are under no compulsion to overwrite in order to fill a leering gap on one page and under no obligation to write at all if we're totally unable to think of enough information to make even a showing on the next. An important feature of a loose-leaf journal is that it permits us to revise and reject as well as just keep adding material. We should think of a journal as forever—consider it as a friend who will follow us right to the end of our writing careers. It will even permit us to throw parts of it out from time to time when we realize they are really quite juvenile and irrelevant.

My journal-keeping method I consider to be simplicity itself. I pass it along to you for your consideration. To begin with, I prefer a selection of common, ordinary twenty-five-cent school exercise books with pictures of farmers harvesting wheat or ships sailing the main on their covers. They make no insistent nagging demands. I use them when I'm in the mood. To make them sound better, let's refer to the exercise books as our *Continuing Journal, a Personal Compendium of Useful, and Often Useless Information* and decide from the outset we'll use it only for entering information or ideas that have at least some remote possibility of being useful when our writing days begin. My journal serves as a data bank on which I make calls when in need. It would help, I'm sure, if it were more carefully and properly indexed, but it's good enough for me. I try, however, to arrange my entries in some logical sequence so that I won't have to pore through dozens of volumes to find some four- or five-line item.

Your *"journal-istic"* habits will develop as you go along. It would be a good idea, perhaps, to devote your first journal entirely to material related to that short story, poem, magazine article, or novel you haven't the time to write. Keep all extraneous matter out. Put that in *another* journal. Begin with a rough outline of the story as you see it, much the same way you've set it up in its unfinished form. Then, from time to time, when you get a new idea or run across some information you think adds to your narration, fill it in. You're really building a storehouse for the future.

Journals have a great tendency to grow and often become unwieldy. Their keepers become as squirrel-like as people who just can't dump old books or magazines or newspapers. They end up with bookshelves overflowing onto tables and chairs and eventually the floor. It'll make your future easier if you learn how to discard and become truly discriminating. When you don't feel like writing, tidy. Organize. Throw out. Edit your gleanings and discard what's outdated. But do so with care.

EDITING ONE'S MEMORIES

It's not easy to edit one's lifetime memories. I have in my files a little ten-line item I plucked out of a newspaper some thirty or forty years ago. It's about a farm in England where a lovely crop of grass was found growing on the sheep's backs. I've been waiting ever since for a way in which I could use this fascinating scrap of knowledge in something I was writing—and have never succeeded till now. I can throw it away at last, satisfied it has served a purpose and no longer sits there tantalizingly staring at me every time I open the page.

The item about grass-growing sheep did serve me in one other way. It was the beginning of a file labeled "Interesting but Useless," which I keep in the metal cabinet by my side. Bulging at the seams, it contains a miscellaneous collection of information for which I am unable to find any other classification. Some of its contents provide satisfying conversation pieces though they will seldom go any farther than that.

I began journal keeping and alphabetical filing long after I was sixty-five. That was when I became serious about writing a book a year, instead of just hopping about writing when I felt like it and scrambling in libraries and newspaper offices and among relatives' private papers for information about whatever topic I had chosen on the spur of the moment. It dawned on me very late that while I'd always written for fun, and had no intention of stopping doing so, the projects I was now about to undertake were also in the nature of a business. If I was in business, I needed to be organized.

What I learned in my late sixties, I'll pass on to you in your thirties or forties and suggest that you save a lot of time in the future by organizing your writing life now.

Here's my system. It's not perfect, I'm sure. But it works for me and could work for you.

GETTING ORGANIZED

First, I decide what subject I'm going to write about. (Basically, I'm a nonfiction writer, though I've managed to get one novel off my chest and have another one inside fighting to get out—later perhaps, when I'm a little older and more mature!) Oddly, it was the novel, not a nonfiction book, that got my organization system working.

I may have two or three subjects in mind at the same time and it's a race to see which one gathers the most moss first. For each of them, I get a nice, fat exercise book (in one case, a loose-leaf) and divide it into sections with headings covering different aspects of the subject. Two years ago, for instance, one of my subjects was the islands of Montreal. Most people know that Montreal itself is an island; what they don't know is that it is part of the St. Lawrence Archipelago consisting of more than thirty islands, each with its own characteristics, people, and history. I spent the better part of two months visiting different islands, talking to inhabitants, studying their history and exploring their landscapes. I decided it was too big to tackle—it would almost need a small encyclopedia. Meanwhile I have sitting in my files thirty or forty

almost empty file folders, each with the name of a different island. Had I not proceeded with the project in an orderly way, I
might well have got so involved that I could have wasted a year's
efforts before giving up.

When a subject notebook grows at a less alarming rate and the
subject is not overwhelming, I begin by having an opening section in which I enter a tentative title, a paragraph or two outlining
what the book is to be about, and a short synopsis—maybe even a
tentative listing of chapters.

Next, I start a section in which I list possible sources for the in
formation I'm going to need. Who can I talk to, write to, or read
about? I need this information early, because correspondence
takes time. If I'm halfway through a book before I write to some
authority in Louisiana, for instance, for information, I must ei‑
ther stop working on the book altogether, jump over the chapter
needing his information, or sit back and wait. Obviously it's not
possible to know all potential sources when one starts; it is a list
that will grow as one's knowledge widens. But, as much as I'm
able, I like to get my information lines busy before I begin to
write.

Now, for an actual illustration of a working journal at work.

In 1970, I retired and moved from a big city to a small town as
remarkable for its lack of civilized debauchery as for its pictur-
esque nineteenth century architecture. Its inhabitants' principal
occupation was sitting; next, during the summer season, it was
lawn bowling, a quasi-athletic activity that most people associ-
ate with old age and that I believed (mistakenly, as it turned out)
had gone the way of the dodo and disappeared about the same
time as my paternal great-grandfather.

Intrigued by the white-attired participants in action (if, indeed,
their leisurely rolling of little balls towards an even littler one,
called a "jack," can be so described) I decided to join them and become a lawn bowling participant. About the same time, the village of which I had become a resident became embroiled in a con-
troversy between old-timers and newcomers over the construction of a three-story "high rise" apartment house on a street of
hundred-year-old mansions.

What would happen, I thought to myself one night as I waited
to bowl, if a big city developer set eyes on our village and decided

to put a shopping plaza, apartment, office tower, or hotel complex right smack on the best site in town—the bowling green owned by the municipality? There was my story, the plot for my very first novel.

I opened section one in my planning book and began making notes. I pictured the villagers rallying 'round to save their precious bowling green, so the title suggested itself: *Rally Round the Jack.* I knew there would be divisions in the ranks of both pro- and anti-builders so I began listing those whom I'd expect to find on each side, using people I knew in the village but giving them different names. Then I realized that I didn't really know much about lawn bowling or lawn bowlers or building developers either, certainly not enough to write a whole book about them. All I knew was enough to list the bowlers as the "good guys" and the developers as the "bad guys." Before I could begin writing, I had a good deal of research to do.

I began by finding out all I could about the history of lawn bowling—in England where it originated and in my village. For such a pleasant, relaxing sport, I discovered, it had a turbulent, often violent history. Banned by kings and Parliaments and denounced by the church, it was condemned as an excuse for gambling, wenching, and avoiding military training as archers for the Royal armies. Obviously my bowlers would have to be involved in a court case where all these historic precedents could be cited.

I examined my fellow players at the club and decided which ones would become my leading characters. Now another decision: Would my book be serious or funny or a mixture of both? Back to the research and the discovery of anecdotes about lawn bowlers and builders and the uncovering of a host of eccentric villagers and city big shots.

All the time, my journal kept growing. For the first time, I found reports about lawn bowling in newspapers and heard about it on radio. Some of the big regional papers, I learned, even had "bowling editors" or correspondents. From these reports I discovered new sources in other towns and cities and soon had a steady stream of letters coming and going from experts and association officials in Canada and the United States. Long before my journal was complete (it now numbered several sections covering every possible angle of a developer-landowner dispute) I began working on an overall outline for the novel. About six months after I first had the idea for a theme, I closed the journal down except for emergency entries, and began writing the first draft.

All my lawn bowling investigations didn't help me bowl any better, but they sure helped me put a book together that brought me a letter from the president of an international lawn bowling association that read in part: "My wife gave me a copy of your book for Christmas and said I should read it because she said she could identify every lawn bowling character—they all belong to our club!"

ALL SYSTEMS GO
In case you get the fever and decide the stories you have inside are worth developing in the future, here's a quick look at my journal-card file system:

Notebook: Section One: Notes on lawn bowling; the game as it is played where I am a member; the local jargon; description of a game of bowls.

Notebook: Section Two: History of lawn bowling in England, Scotland; notes about similar games in other countries; early game records; court cases in England.

Notebook: Section Three: Characters; notes on descriptions and talks with old-time bowlers; visits to other clubs and conversations; club traditions.

Notebook: Section Four: Anecdotes; books about bowling.

Notebook: Section Five: Building developers, background.

Notebook: Section Six: Takeovers; community conflicts over developments.

File folders: Alphabetical arrangement by subject of folders containing clippings from newspapers and magazines; written correspondence with bowling officials, city clerks, building companies; an index of clippings so they may be found quickly.

Gathering time: approximately one year; no regular schedule, just being constantly on the lookout for related information, names of new sources and following up leads as they come.

Note-making: Probably an hour or so a day; getting down on paper in the proper sections or files information garnered during the previous twenty-four hours.

Writing time: Creating a skeleton, a rather detailed outline of a tentative plot plus descriptions and characterizations.

Final story time: About three months, concluding with about a week of revisions and corrections, checking against notes.

There are other alternatives for those who look with disdain upon printed diaries or school day exercise books. We may do all our note taking on a tape recorder, index our cassettes and keep them in organized compartments on our desks or in desk drawers. We can edit these from time to time, as we do with a journal, erase ones that have become out of date and make simple corrections. The indexing is important if we ever expect to find references when we want them. Or we may trust all to a computer: It has a memory much bigger than ours and, providing we have learned how to program it correctly, can be counted on to tell us everything we want to know, whenever we want it.

No method suits everyone but, after all, it's not the paper or the binding or the plastic tape that matters. It's what we put on them. As Thoreau once told a friend who asked him what he thought about the new telegraph service from Boston to Chicago: "It's not important that someone in Boston can communicate with someone in Chicago. What is important is—Does someone in Boston have anything to say to someone in Chicago?"

A final word: Read a lot. Read the kind of books you'd like to write, books by authors you enjoy and whose writing style appeals to you. Again you may say, "I don't have time." Try reading on buses or airplanes or subway cars, or for half an hour in bed at night—unless you have something more important on your mind.

THREE

A Room, a Desk, a Typewriter, and—Wow!

*I should be glad to have the library to myself
as soon as may be.*

Jane Austen in *Pride and Prejudice*

Forget what you've read about struggling writers starving in unheated garrets (and also forget what you read in gossip columns and see on television about millionaire authors who spend their best-seller royalties on yachts and racing cars and Christian Dior evening gowns). Realize that most professional writers—even the best of them—are underpaid but reasonably well fed, and comfortably if not luxuriously lodged. With a pension or Social Security check as a foundation, you can use your writing to provide extra dividends if you go about it properly in a businesslike fashion.

During the Depression, when I was really poor (not just inflation-poor, like now), I used to fence myself in behind a table and a couple of high-back chairs in a corner of the living room where I felt comfortable because I was out of sight, even though the rest of the family was only seven or eight feet away. There I hauled out my heavy, battered typewriter, sat at a dilapidated desk I'd picked up at a secondhand store, and hammered out a flow of free-lance articles and news stories for *American Weekly*, the *Star Weekly*, *Women's Wear Daily*, *True Confessions*, and a society magazine called *Mayfair*. The dream books and really creative ideas I had inside I didn't have time to work on, but I was still grateful to get those ten-, fifteen-, or twenty-dollar checks.

Even in my cramped quarters, I managed to provide myself with the essentials a professional writer needs, besides a typewriter and stacks of blank paper. It was definitely make-do, entirely unromantic, and I couldn't imagine any writer choosing to work that way unless he had to. Then, forty years later, visiting a friend in London, I found an extremely successful professional writer operating under almost identical circumstances, except that the checks were bigger. Wili Frischauer, biographer of Heinrich Himmler, Jackie Onassis, Princess Margaret, David Frost, Brigitte Bardot, and a dozen other international celebrities, was sitting in an armchair, portable typewriter on an end-table beside him, in a six-by-eight-foot space in the corner of a small London apartment. From there he dispatched a steady flow of manuscripts that became saleable books, feature articles for British and American magazines, and essays on current events for the political and literary press. He was delighted that he needn't rise from his chair to find anything he wanted. Wili achieved privacy and solitude in an area not much larger than a Dalmatian-size dog kennel. His wife, Nickie, clean-typed his manuscripts on the kitchen table. With the proceeds, the two of them traveled Europe and America, stayed at the best hotels, were greeted by name at the world's leading restaurants. They never managed a yacht!

Generally, however, things in the writing world have changed. The appearance of poverty is no longer a prerequisite for proof of genius, so we who revel in pensions and compound interest may properly invest in the trappings that make life more agreeable and, just possibly, more productive.

Begin with the basics. You'll need some equipment for your new activity. But first, and most importantly, you'll need a place to work.

A PRIVATE PLACE

Except for busy newspaper, radio, or TV reporters accustomed to writing in haste in crowded, noisy surroundings (not excluding battlefields), writers as a general rule yearn for quiet and privacy. They may hope that others will want to read or listen to what they write, but they prefer that people don't do it over their shoulders while they're in the process of writing it. They are particularly annoyed by people who insist on carrying on a conversation while they are busy creating.

I think this preference is shared by retirees setting out on their voyages of literary discovery for the first time.

It's true that a writer can write anywhere. Most of them, even if their chosen metier is fiction writing, spend more than half their writing time away from their bases, researching or picking up bits and pieces to write about. Their truly enjoyable period comes when they sit alone, staring into space, twiddling with paper clips, shuffling papers, and finally taking their first tentative taps at a typewriter: "There were fifteen people abroad that night when Jim and Nancy first visited the haunted castle. . . ."

At last, the creative process for which all else was preparation is underway.

Senior Citizen writers have finally found time, the lack of which kept them from becoming complete writers before. In most cases, they'll find their need for privacy may be satisfied as well, even if they move from a large self-contained house into an apartment, a mobile dwelling in a retirement village, or a room in a Senior Citizens' home.

Or they may stay home. And that may need some diplomacy. If, after spending their days in offices and factories, retirees now move into the home full-time, they will, in a way, be intruding on what has been their spouse's domain. Likewise, those who remained at home performing the world's most important unpaid jobs, now relieved of the responsibilities of caring for children, may want to start doing some writing of their own without having to break off every ten minutes to wash socks or produce a sandwich. The readjustment will need tact on both sides: Their marital relationship will already be subjected to unaccustomed stresses and strains by the new situation and doesn't need to be made even more difficult by having the aspiring writer plump himself or herself at the dining room table and begin pounding away at a typewriter, expecting all household chores to be done by the other. Whichever partner is the writer, both will rejoice if the housekeeping can be equitably divided and the writing can be done in a private place.

Others, while still living at home, may go shopping for an office elsewhere. This can sometimes lead to unfortunate results if the whole family's welfare is not taken into account. If the partner left at home alone is the one who's been accustomed to going out to work every day, the isolation that often comes with retirement may be intensified just when added support and companionship are needed. If there are still children in the household, other problems may arise. Take the case of a free-lancer I know. In her fifties, she decided there were too many interruptions at home and rented a small office in a nearby shopping center. Her two teenaged children, suddenly released from after-school parental supervision, took to drugs and ended up in a reformatory. That part-time Senior career ended in tragedy. Before we go off by ourselves to pursue our dreams, we need to give some thought to what we're leaving behind, all by *itself*, while we're away.

The writing craft is often criticized for being a "solitary occupation," good only for hermits or self-centered egomaniacs who turn their backs on society. Still, there is some merit, even in today's all-too-public society, in being able to think and dream and create and find companionship within oneself. Thoreau found that merit at Walden Pond and wrote: "I never found the companion that was so companionable as solitude. We are for the most part more lonely when we go abroad among men than when we stay in our chambers. A man thinking or working is always alone, let him be where he will." David Reisman, in his book *The Lonely Crowd*, said much the same thing.

CHOOSING YOUR FURNITURE

Your newfound private corner—whether it be one end of the family living room, a vestibule in the upper hall, a second bedroom that's been a den, studio, or workshop or whatever you decided to call it, or in the basement family room where the kids used to romp while you were working overtime at the office or were upstairs trying to get caught up on the laundry—wherever it is, that's your *office*, as of now: your own writing workshop. You're entitled to hang a "please do not disturb" sign on the door or curtain and expect family, friends, and drop-in visitors to respect an aging person at work.

In your office, you're going to put a few basic tools. These items you *should* acquire at once. I hesitate to say *must* because you'll immediately tell me about the Carolina author who lives in a treehouse and sells a short story a month to a national magazine. Let's just stay with the *should* and trust that you're a more or less normal human being who has just retired from the hectic world of stocks and bonds or the computerized, automated factory floor and are not about to become a Bohemian hack or a Vincent Price in a book-lined library with Tiffany lamps. You'll be satisfied with a comfortable place to think and work.

You *should* have a desk, or table, large enough to accommodate papers and folders, pen and pencil containers, telephone number-finders, memo pads, a perpetual calendar, and maybe a clock. Paper clips and rubber bands are also nice to play with and are sometimes useful. No matter how large your desk or table is, it will never be quite large enough to accommodate all the books, papers, documents, scraps and bits and pieces you will use when you're actually writing. Be prepared for a certain amount of disorder. It doesn't mean you're untidy, even though your partner, or whoever's responsible for feeding you and making sure you get some fresh air once a day, may say that you are.

Next comes a comfortable office chair adjusted to your shape and size—a swivel, if possible, so you won't strain your back when you're trying to reach a notebook a tantalizing three inches out of reach behind you. If you know a secretary or stenographer, past or present, ask advice about posture chairs. Otherwise, try used office furniture suppliers and test their merchandise by sitting in it.

Seated in one of these scientifically designed pieces of furniture, you'll be able to spend quite long hours typing without having to hustle off to a chiropractor to have your spine reactivated.

A good desk lamp that can be made to direct the light toward what you're reading or writing is a sensible precaution against eyestrain. I also use a small plastic desk easel to hold pages I am copying.

This may seem to have little to do with your writing, but if you're going to be able to complete your manuscripts and then be in shape to battle editorial demands for changes and corrections and "hurry up with the revisions, we want to go to press," you'd be wise to pay some attention to your physical condition. If it hurts to write, you're not going to write. So get comfortable!

YOUR TYPEWRITER

A good, workable typewriter is the next essential item—unless, of course, you intend to dictate what you "write" and let someone else do the typing. While you may like to write, as Dickens did, with a quill pen, editors who will be asked to buy your work have no such romantic notions and show a distinct preference for copy that is typewritten. Too bad, but as far as professional writing is concerned, calligraphy is a lost art, and you will no more be expected to submit your prose or poetry tied with pretty red ribbons than will you be required to wear a black flowing cape and beret while composing.

The typewriter you buy should probably be a standard office-sized model. The bigger machines are preferable to most portables, which bounce about a bit particularly if, like me, you're a three-finger typist. Electric portables are better because they're not only heavier but easier to use, once you get accustomed to their lighter-touch keys. If you're not using an old or inherited machine and are shopping for a new or reconditioned one, opt for pica rather than elite type. Again, editors prefer it and what you like or dislike may be secondary. And don't be persuaded to buy a machine that prints in italics; don't even accept one as a gift from a grandchild. Editors abhor them. Unless you delight in wasting time trying to unravel typewriter ribbons every time you have to change them, I'd also suggest getting a machine that uses ribbon cartridges and has an automatic eraser. That's one modern invention I appreciate. What'll they think of next?

What they'll think of—and already have—is computers, which come to the writing profession as word processors. They're that rare thing which some writer once said didn't exist—something new under the sun. I'll talk about them in a minute. Meanwhile, let's return to more mundane things, like paper.

YOUR PAPER

There are expert advisers who will tell you exactly what weight of typewriter paper, what size envelope, and what manner of stick-on labels you should use. One of those authorities whose message I read recently said writers should have printed letterhead to show that they're professionals. Next, they'll be suggesting that before you start to write, you have an industrial graphic designer concoct your logo. I may be wrong, but I think it highly unlikely that John Updike, Pulitzer Prize winner Alice Walker, or any other successful author you'd care to name sent their manuscripts out on printed letterhead; yet they managed to get editorial attention and acceptance. Some writers are just born lucky, I guess. Anyway, I don't have a printed letterhead and I don't care much about the weight or shade of paper I use. Like Henry Ford, who told buyers they could buy their Model A's in any color provided it was black, I give editors a choice of any color for my manuscript paper provided it's white.

I fancy that editors are most accustomed to receiving manuscripts on some kind of bond paper that's 8½ x11 inches, neatly typewritten and double spaced; I doubt they ever go to the trouble to weigh the paper to see if it comes up to expectations. Nor could they care less if a manuscript arrives in a brown 5x7 envelope or a perfumed magenta 11x14 with gold edges, except they'll throw the envelope away faster if it's tinted or perfumed—and probably your manuscript with it. Stick to white.

I'm a traditionalist and have never yet had my copy delivered to an editor by a singing delivery person, though perhaps if you can't get by the mail desk any other way, that might be worth a try. Stranger things have happened and will continue to happen in the publishing world.

I have a confession to make. Once, in a display of unusual editorial cunning, I had painted on the backs of baby turtles a message inviting certain editors and advertising executives to a sales conference. The little creatures, for whom at last a sensible use had been found, were mailed in boxes stuffed with seaweed and what the dealer said was desiccated turtle food. This new editorial approach aroused the ire of the local humane society, which alerted the press but ended happily when it was learned that most of the turtles survived and were well cared for in their recipients' offices. Attendance at the conference set a new record.

But as a general rule, being businesslike is better. "Cute" or "fancy" approaches can backfire—and that includes putting smiley faces (or any other such "appealing" little scribbles) in the margins.

One thing for sure: You'll need paper if you intend to write anything. Make sure to have a good supply always on hand. Nothing is more annoying or disconcerting than to find you've used the last sheet just when you're firing away and getting to the climax. The same goes for copy paper and carbons—though again, some writers recommend photocopying manuscripts. Photocopying can be expensive at ten or fifteen cents a page, and inconvenient since you've got to go to the library, a post office, or some print shop to get the use of a machine. And half the time the one you want to use either has a lineup of teenagers copying exam questions or is out of order.

There's another small advantage to making carbon copies. I always use a colored paper—yellow, blue, or green—so that when they are in my files and the original is out on the road, I can pull out the one I want right away without having to read title or heading. You're never likely to be working on more than two or three manuscripts at a time (my record is four), so the system is simple. Make the carbons of your dog story on yellow paper, those of your atom bomb article on blue, and your novel's carbons on green. That's not hard to remember, and it's no great feat to spot the color you want on your desk or in a file. Colored folders or bright folder labels might do just as well.

It's important that you keep a copy of any original manuscript: Never have an original floating around in the mail without having a facsimile of it secure at home. And, talking about security, I'm a bug for protection and therefore deposit my carbon copy, as chapters are completed, in a safe-deposit box. Then I can be sure that if my house burns down or some nut breaks in and scatters furniture and filing cabinets far and wide, I'll have a complete manuscript on hand and not have to start all over again. Since most home offices are far from fire- or burgler-proof, it might also be a good idea to deposit one's notes in the safe-deposit box till you're ready to use them. No insurance company will pay you for more than the cost of the typing and paper if your work gets destroyed or lost. Unsold manuscripts have little value in the eyes of the relentless insurance adjuster.

I seem to be writing an awful lot about paper. But paper today is expensive (what isn't?) so I save it where I can. When I'm writing a book, I'll write maybe three or four complete drafts of each chapter. That adds up to more than a thousand sheets in all. When I finish draft number two, rendering draft number one obsolete, I don't destroy the first one. I simply run a line diagonally across the now-useless copy, so I won't get mixed up with a later draft (that's why I also keep colored pencils handy), turn the sheets over, and use the backs for draft number three. Presto! A thousand sheets are reduced to five hundred.

Very well-known authors often (in fact, usually) keep their originals and draft copies and either sell them or give them to universities or other institutions that specialize in collecting authors' manuscripts. Some of these become very valuable and are worth more than the published books. Imagine, for instance, that you owned an original Shakespeare folio or a corrected text by Mark Twain! I have no such illusions and think it even less likely that editors, critics, or librarians of the future will fight to secure copies of my literary works than that today's editors will fight to publish them. So, once in print, the original manuscript goes on the shelf for perhaps a year, assuming that the publisher even sends it back; then, along with any carbon copies, it's dumped.

If you think you've got a best seller or a book that will be cherished by scholars, then by all means hang on to your working papers, draft copies, and original manuscripts. There's nothing like getting paid twice for the same work. Or you can always recycle it by the pound.

HANDY EXTRAS: STAMPS, NOTEBOOKS, FILES, AND A BOOKCASE

Now, what else do you need? A stamp container with compartments for different denominations should be kept well stocked, though buying by the roll is no longer the small investment it used to be. In Canada, 100 first-class stamps cost thirty-two dollars; in the United States, twenty-two dollars as of this moment, though it may well have gone up again while you turned the page. And a single first-class stamp is never nearly enough to pay for a manuscript, not counting the return postage you're always going to include with any manuscript you send out, doubling the amount. Therefore, keep a good supply on hand and you'll save trotting back and forth to the post office every time you have a letter or manuscript to mail. You'll save more time, and money, if you have a postal scale and keep a set of postal rates handy, so you don't stick on even a penny's worth of postage you don't need to. And, since the material will be all ready, you won't need to go any farther than the nearest mailbox to start it on its way.

Next, if you're going to be truly businesslike in all phases of your writing, you'll need a supply of standard-size notebooks and a filing cabinet big enough to hold folders with information and correspondence, both of which will accumulate at an alarming rate if you're a diligent reader or listener. A bookcase within easy reach, holding at least one good dictionary, a Roget's thesaurus (so you won't scream with frustration when you can't think of another word for "however"), a book of collected quotations, and reference books about the subject or subjects you are currently writing about, is more than just a luxury.

KEEPING YOUR ACCOUNTS

Finally, you will need an account book or ledger in which you can keep track of legitimate writing expenses which may be deducted from your writing income for tax purposes. To learn what are legitimate expenses (you may, for instance, deduct a percentage of your rent, or mortgage payments, heating and electricity bills, telephone, etc.), you might consult an accountant or join one of the writers' associations which supply that kind of information for members. The problem is that you must have had something published to be eligible for membership in organizations such as the National Writers' Union (U.S.) or the Writer's Union of Canada. So until you qualify, you might want to read *Writers' Legal and Business Guide* by Norman Bell, or *Law and the Writer*, edited by Kirk Polking and Leonard S. Meranus. And you might also look in the *Reader's Guide to Periodical Literature* in the reference section of your library to find the newest articles which have been printed on the subject. They'll tell you what's involved in claiming a home office, what's deductible and what's not, what receipts and records you need to keep, and whatever else you'd need to know.

CONGRATULATIONS: YOU'RE A SECRETARY!

Once you're on your own, properly housed, as it were, and eager to get to work, you'll find a big difference between working alone as a self-employed writer and being part of a team or business organization. There'll be no one there to make sure you start and stop on time, keep proper records, or produce what you've "hired" yourself to produce. And you're going to have to learn about office practices and services you never knew about before.

Writers, as a rule, have no secretaries or assistants popping up on demand to produce documents, reports, letters—or coffee, except weary spouses who are often expected to be sounding boards as well as messengers and proofreaders. Writing is not only a lonely occupation, it's one that is poorly serviced. You'll have to become your own girl or boy Friday, answer your own phone calls and take down your own messages. Unless, of course, you're retired on a more than comfortable income and want to do this writing thing up in executive style.

You may also be a high tech fan and are preparing to live in, work with, and possibly write about a robot-dominated world. Or let's say that you're not that rich or high tech-minded, but you have confidence in your ability to sell what you write and want to get on with the job in the quickest, most efficient way. Right away, you hire an answering service for your phone, or attach the mechanical kind that goes "beep!" and records the messages on tape. That's one problem solved. Then you investigate your nearest computer dealer and decide to order a word processor. Now, you've either solved a lot of problems or created a number of new ones—likely, both. You are on the verge of joining the writing world's elite—the men and women who can afford and will accept nothing but the best. No more talk about Fords and postage stamps: You're about to acquire a writer's equivalent of a Mercedes or a Ferrari.

DO YOUR WORDS NEED PROCESSING?
ONLY YOU CAN TELL.

Many "old-fashioned" writers who continue to produce best sellers and have incomes well over $100,000 refuse to have anything to do with computers and prefer to do all their creative work on a typewriter (not even an electric one) or, in extreme cases, by hand. Some of them believe modern technology gets in the way and turns the writer into some kind of mechanic. Others are probably just too lazy to abandon a system that has worked pretty well for them and they don't want to go back to school or leaf through instruction manuals—which they'll have to do if they're going to learn to run one of those newfangled machines.

At the same time, there are many writers whose names are well known and hundreds, if not thousands, of journalists who swear that a word processor is a writer's best friend. In editorial departments of virtually every major newspaper and magazine in America, these stylish and ubiquitous machines have replaced what were considered the last word in copy writing devices only a decade or so ago. Newsrooms once were occupied by rows of desks where news hawks and rewrite editors batted out reams of copy, often in short "takes," a paragraph at a time. Copy boys or girls stood by waiting to grab the hot copy as it came off the typewriters and rush it to the copy desk for final editing. Today, the news writers tap (almost) silently on keyboards and gaze into miniature screens watching their flow of words appear as lines of type. If a mistake appears, or a reporter wants to change what was written, the word processor makes it easy to fix what's wrong and to shift words, lines, or paragraphs around however the reporter wants.

Journalists also retire, as do engineers, lighting designers, supermarket clerks, secretaries, doctors, dentists, and crane operators: people who have been using sophisticated machinery all their working lives. For the many Seniors with high tech backgrounds, the fact that a machine is unfamiliar won't necessarily be a reason to dislike it. For them and for the many other Seniors who are simply "gadgety," who found that just pushing typewriter keys made them want to write, a word processor can seem the most delightful toy they've ever had their hands on. Others will feel, just as rightly, that learning one new skill—writing—at a time is quite enough without learning a whole new way of making letters appear on paper besides.

If a word processor seems too drastic or too costly an investment as basic, start-up equipment, you might consider settling for an electronic typewriter as one short step into the high tech world. Electronic typewriters have two principal advantages over the ordinary machine. They operate silently—a handicap in my house where my wife has become so accustomed to typewriter clacking over more than fifty years that if she doesn't hear it, she thinks I've gone to sleep. And they have "memories," but more limited ones than do word processors, that let you go back a few words and make changes or corrections as you're typing. Depending on the model you buy, an electronic typewriter will remember fifteen or twenty letters and, at the tap of a special key, move backward through the text and let you make the change, then return to the place where you left off.

Whether high tech equipment can increase or improve your writing or not depends more on you than on the device you use. It will certainly increase your vocabulary: you'll become familiar with words like PIP, SYSGEN, and bytes, boots, and buffers. You won't have to speak "tech" to use the machine, any more than you have to know what a carburetor does to drive a car; but what's the use of having all this expensive equipment if you can't show off a little?

Recently I had lunch with an elderly gentleman who lives in a retirement home nearby. "I was very lucky," he said. "When I was a boy, my father insisted I go to business school and learn typing and shorthand. I have never lost those abilities to put my thoughts on paper." He's eighty-two years old now and it's more than sixty years since he learned how to type properly, using all ten fingers and thumbs. During that time, he has written just a few poems and only now is he playing with the idea of writing his life story.

I never went to business college, never learned shorthand, and I type with all three fingers—two on the right hand, one on the left, keeping my thumbs carefully curled up and out of the way so they won't accidentally tap the electric keyboard. In just short of sixty adult years, I've written more than twenty published books, several hundred articles in newspapers and magazines, and countless news releases and reviews. Would I have written more if I'd learned to type properly? Or would my old friend have written more if he had thought more about what he had to say than how clever he was at typing it? Who knows?

If you're receptive to modern technology, have the money to spend, and don't expect your computer to pay for itself in the first five years, by all means treat yourself to a word processor, take the necessary lessons to learn how to operate it, and join the oncoming Pepsi generation..

There's no doubt that once you master the thing—without letting it become more interesting in itself than what you have to say—a word processor can do a lot for you and for your manuscripts. As the operating system of a home computer, a word processor may serve a multitude of purposes. It can be your memory bank, saving you the trouble of keeping a lot of messy notes. If what you put in it in the first place was right, you can count on its being absolutely accurate whenever you look at it again. And if it wasn't right, it's easy to change. Most word processing programs can identify typing and spelling mistakes in your copy and, when you need to make corrections, insertions, or deletions, will shift chunks of text around with lightning speed. With no strikeovers or erasures, no paste-ups or white-outs, you'll have a manuscript that would delight even the ubiquitous Mr. Clean. And extra copies emerge from your printer anytime you need them, every page faultless.

If you enjoy playing with a processor and it attracts you to your workshop, by all means get one. After all, you'll be no different than the retired woodworking hobbyist who has realized *his* or *her* great dream by having a shop loaded with the latest Black and Decker tools that measure, cut, adjust, plane, and polish at the flick of a switch and allow their owners to be 100 percent creative. Try to get any one of them to go back to a handsaw and a hand-operated drill!

It really isn't important whether you see yourself as a pioneer in the computerized writing field or as an old fuddy duddy resisting change. What's important is that you write. Whatever makes your writing easier, more effective, or more fun will help you get more writing done. What you'll end up with, however you produce them, are words on a page. And only the words really matter.

WHAT IS A WORD PROCESSOR?

Now, just to make sure you get some value out of these ramblings about computers and word processing programs, I hied myself off to see a writer who has become a computer addict and she told me everything she thought I needed to know about the subject. Her final conclusion: "I wouldn't do without it. It makes my writing fun." Unfortunately, those last two sentences were the only ones

I understood during a two-hour conversation. I could as well carry on a talk in Urdu as in computer-ese.

Then, by chance, I ran across a fascinating article called "My Pal the Computer" by Bob Lane, who seemed like a sensible person and who was obviously less under the spell of the technological world's gift to writers. His article, addressed to Seniors who might covet a word processor either for writing letters or manuscripts or simply to impress their Juniors, appeared in the magazine *Dynamic Years*, published by the American Association of Retired Persons.

Lane begins by pointing out that if you plan to use your computer setup for processing manuscripts or letters and readying them for mailing to editors, you need both a word processor and a printer. The computer (that little keyboard hitched to a miniature TV-type screen), using a word processing program (a set of instructions telling it what to do), lines up your sentences, makes your corrections, and enables you to produce a clean piece of copy on the screen. The printer transfers to paper whatever you have composed on the screen, giving you the thing you are going to mail—with additional copies as required.

According to my own research, a word processing system can cost anywhere from $3,000 to $4,000 and up, although some of my writing friends tell me some of the newest, most compact systems sell for as little as $400 or $500, not counting the printer or any "peripherals" (accessories). Lane says a high-quality printer that will print more than one double-spaced page a minute can cost another $1,000 to $2,000. But for writers who don't need that much speed, Lane suggests choosing a slower, less expensive model. Whatever kind of printer you buy, be sure it's "letter quality." Editors don't like to go blind squinting at collections of tiny dots masquerading as the alphabet. Some threaten to return "dot-matrix" prints without even reading them. So don't risk that!

If you're to own and operate a word processor, Lane continues, you "should have the temperament for self-instruction. For all practical purposes, you must learn your skill by yourself. No college course, book salesman, or friend can be expected to know the intricacies of your particular lash-up [see what I mean about language?] of computer, printer, and software. The instructions for my SC printer run 35 pages; my KayPro printer's instructions are

504 pages long; the heart of my system, the WordStar word processing software [program] tells me all I want to know in 186 pages plus a 96-page training guide. That's 821 pages in all, weighing in at around 12 pounds."

When you are just becoming acquainted with your new processor, be prepared for sudden disasters. You can spend all Sunday afternoon setting up your copy, have everything ship-shape, then "all of a sudden you come to computerdom's most common transgression: You press the wrong button.

"The screen goes ape. One line of figures flies off the left screen; the cursor (the little blinking thing that tells you where you are on the screen) will not budge, and the manual is infuriatingly silent about how to rectify a wrong command. . . . Be warned: The frustration level at a computer terminal equals or surpasses [that at] the golf course."

If you decide to shop for a word processor, prepare yourself well for the expedition. Pick up manufacturers' brochures, read whatever basic literature about computers is available at the library or bookstore, and do what the wonderful old Packard Motor Company used to tell prospective buyers to do: "Ask the man who owns one." Neighbors, friends, or grandchildren may have a system they'd be just tickled to show off to you and let you tinker around with. Twenty lessons in computer-ese won't teach you as much as the feel of your fingers on the keyboard, making words appear.

Remember, the computer industry is still comparatively new and there are hundreds of dealers who are in-and-outers, in for the quick buck. In the automobile market, you can still buy a lemon or get tied up with a dealer who gives lousy maintenance service. The risk in computer buying is greater. Some dealers offer free instruction for a new buyer. Find out how many hours, and who's the instructor. What happens if you get in a jam and need help? Ask for some names and phone numbers of satisfied users. Don't be impressed with all the things a system will do that you don't really want done. Decide beforehand, from your reading, what abilities you'd really find handy in a system and which ones are just frills, like automatic windows or a stereo system in a car, that you can do as well without.

Lane concludes his article with a nice little cautionary anecdote. The first two articles he produced on his processor were models of neatness. As he put them in the mailbox, he writes, "I rather pitied those freelancers out there who didn't have my competitive advantage." But, alas, "both manuscripts were rejected within the week by first line editors using rejection slips. I may still write junk, but at least it's neat junk." Modest Mr. Lane makes an important point when he explains that editors buy information and good writing, not just good typing. A computer will help you type; it won't help you write.

Forty-odd years ago, I gave up buying Christmas trees because the setting-up process, including lights and simplified metal stands, became so complicated that I was a physical and mental wreck hours before Santa Claus was due. For the same reason, I gave up buying any appliance or piece of furniture that was delivered in pieces, leaving me the task of putting them together. And for the same reason again, I've given up word processors and computers in general without even trying them. Three fingers, get to work! Hammer a little harder and my Smith-Corona is good for another ten years. Wish I could say the same for me.

One more small piece of advice: Whatever mechanical equipment you buy, lease, or rent, you'll be well advised to purchase a service contract for it, one that includes pickup and delivery (to save your back) and in-home service, if whatever's wrong with your machine can be fixed on the spot. All writing machines deserve and need an annual cleaning—more frequent ones, if you use them a lot. Cartridge-type correction ribbons leave a residue of white lint which clogs the keys; and keys do break and wear out, no matter how light your touch. You'll be happier if someone comes in once or twice a year and does a checkup; and, since breakdowns always occur just when you're in the middle of a most important manuscript, it's comforting if your contract calls for a replacement on loan if and when major repairs are required.

BE YOUR OWN BEST EMPLOYEE

Long ago, employers discovered that employees were more productive working in pleasant surroundings and provided with efficient tools and equipment. Now, after fifty, if we are to become writers, whether full- or part-time, we will be self-employed. We'll want to keep up our productivity and at the same time maintain an economic balance. If we can work in a shed or basement room with a manual typewriter, or just pen and ink, fine. Lots of great writers have done just that. If we feel we'll do better in an executive suite surrounded by the latest products of modern technology, that's just fine, too. All we'll need is money. Caution, however, is recommended.

Be businesslike. Don't buy more than you need and can use, especially in the beginning. Check out the classified ads and the used business equipment stores. Don't buy expensive if cheaper will do. Starting out with something new, we have to keep our feet on the ground, not let our expectations run so high that initial market rejections could destroy all the pleasure we have in the writing itself.

Think of the hundreds of restaurants that open every year, their optimistic owners spending hundreds of thousands of dollars on decor and fine china and heading for bankruptcy before their potential clients have discovered the simply marvelous quality of their food. The same thing may happen to a beginning writer who spends all his money and too much of his time engineering an atmosphere where he or she can create and too little time creating.

If and when you sell something you've written, that's the time to celebrate and indulge yourself—with a nicer desk, a better typewriter, a word processor . . . or maybe a few restaurant dinners or a vacation in the sun.

And in the meantime, enjoy yourself.

I am one who believes that for people who genuinely like to write, the joy of writing may well be reward enough. But as a Senior Citizen who must live on a couple of minor pensions that looked just great in the sixties and will barely pay the grocery bill in the eighties, and on the interest from what small savings my wife and I accumulated during forty years of hard labor, I have come to attach considerable importance to the monetary returns which may accrue from exercising what I once considered primarily a hobby. Writing will never make me rich; nor is it likely to perform that delightful service for many retired persons who are now free to test their writing skills in the marketplace. For them, as for me, doing what we like to do may become even more agreeable if it pays a dividend every once in a while.

FOUR

Get Ready—Get Set—Go!

Great is the art of beginning.

Henry Wadsworth Longfellow

Here we are, all settled down in our new private place, removed from the madding crowd, soon to be free from the pressures of middle age. We're seated in our comfortable chair, facing a desk liberally littered with the accoutrements of our newfound craft, flanked by a typewriter (or word processor) and a shelf of reference books. Staring at us balefully is a mountain of plain white paper sheets waiting to be filled. Our try-out period is beginning; during the next few years, we'll begin to get our feet wet and discover if writing is to play a major part in our retirement years. Away ahead, in our own private dreamland, is our first published book or article or poem.

This is to be our Golden Age—the era we've been waiting for, lo these many years, to accomplish the great literary feats we were too busy to undertake before. Our time is near: the moment of truth. Are we, or are we not, to be writers? If we are, surely words should be pouring forth from our re-activated brains as we rush to say what we've held back so long.

It's strange, but even when we're sixty-five or seventy, we won't feel so different from the way we felt years ago. There'll be the same old desire to procrastinate, to put off until some later date what we've been putting off all our adult lives. Arriving at sixty-five, the official entry point for retirees, will bring about no miraculous transformation; the only thing that will have changed will be we won't have the same excuse we had when we were young. We'll no longer be too busy to write, and perhaps we never really were. Passage of years is not necessarily going to change our habits or remedy all our faults. As Thomas Mann said in *The Magic Mountain:* "Time has no divisions to mark its passage; there is never a thunderstorm or a blare of trumpets to announce the beginning of a new month or year. Even when a new century begins, it is only we mortals who ring bells and fire off pistols."

We'll still be what we were, hair a little whiter, faces a little more wrinkled. If anyone's going to ring bells or fire off pistols, it will have to be us.

TIME ENOUGH FOR EVERYTHING BUT WASTING

We're past the pure fantasy stage now, the period when we wanted to write a short story or perhaps a novel or a series of articles about gliding "if we only had time." Face facts: We're about to have the time. Don't dig out your old files and say: "I'm too old to start writing now. I should have done it when I was young." We're all as young as we feel, or as we want to be, in spite of those occasional twinges that keep reminding us we're no longer sweet sixteen or the junior member of the firm. We have to stop thinking that we're too tired; of course we are, but well-scheduled afternoon naps can remedy that. How do you think the seventy-five-year-old Winston Churchill felt after late-night sessions of the war cabinet and afternoon rows in Parliament? He felt just fine, because he learned how to cat-nap at any free hour of the day or night.

Our minds won't stop working unless we let them, and one way to make sure they don't is to give them something to do. Let's find out if we have the talent or the story-telling gift that will go with it. If we do, we can make the next decades of our lives a creative experience which may be financially rewarding as well.

TAKING STOCK

There are two closely related questions we must ask ourselves. Do we have anything to say that might conceivably interest any other living being? And *what* do we want to write about? The answers to these questions will go a long way to determining whether or not a writing career is in the cards for us. And the answers must come from within. No one has yet arrived to tell us what we should be doing or how we should go about it. That will come later, when we ourselves have decided that the game is worth the candle and that we are prepared to accept the challenge and ready to reap the rewards that will come if we master the writing craft.

Let's approach our never-too-late entry into the world realistically and examine our assets and liabilities as potential writers. Then we may chart the course we wish to follow.

STEP ONE:

We dig back into the records we brought with us from our former life and haul out that short story, novel, family history, or article we always said we hadn't had time to finish. We thought at one time that it was just what the world was waiting for and that, given the proper opportunity (meaning financial security), we could quit our job or hire someone to look after our homes and be right up there on the best-seller lists. We could even see our pictures, a little hazily perhaps, in the Books Section of the *New York Times.*

Well, the world's been waiting twenty or thirty years. Do we still think we have an unfinished symphony? Or are we a little doubtful and think perhaps it's just a bit of doggerel? Should we get some professional advice first? Or, worse, could we consider dumping the whole idea and taking up wind-surfing or raising hamsters? Are we fully aware of the work, the time, and the frustration involved in creating even a tiny masterpiece? How determined are we to see the thing through if we once get started?

If, after reading what we wrote when we were thirty and dabbled in for two decades, we still think it has merit and we'd like to finish it and then move on to further creative efforts, how do we go about that?

(a) Do we pick up the article, story, or play where we left off and run it through to a conclusion? Fashions in writing, like everything else, change; the research we did in our thirties may be all out of date in the eighties; five other pieces on much the same subject may have been brought out recently by the very publisher we were thinking of contacting. Perhaps our story would have been bubbling with timeliness in 1964 but has since suffered the fate of leftover champagne. Perhaps a little study of today's literary output would be helpful in reaching a decision because in writing, as in car designing, there's very little profit in bucking the trend. You don't want to labor for weeks, months, or years to produce a 1980's Edsel.

Louise Boggess, who knows more about writing and selling short stories than most professional authors and is the author of *How to Write Short Stories that Sell,* thinks we should take a really hard look at that twenty-five or thirty-year-old manuscript. "Unless an idea inspires and challenges you to give it your creative best," she writes, "discard it. Sometimes a writer becomes so attached to an idea through long hours of trying to develop it into a story that he not only refuses to discard it but will balk at parting with a single precious word." Maybe those words and sentences we've been hoarding and facts we've been assembling should be a write-off. Certainly if it's nonfiction we're planning to write, we'd better either begin seriously re-researching our subject, or else we should . . .

(b) start all over again, with a fresh approach and a fresh point of view, but following the same general theme. We'd still be like a dog chewing an old bone, but our teeth would be sharper. We'd see our characters a little more clearly and we'd have had a couple of decades or more of experiences to strengthen our perception and widen our plots; we'd have had a wider context in which to place present facts and trends. Maybe beginning *from* the beginning would be the best way.

STEP TWO:
We evaluate our writing skills.

"A man," G. K. Chesterton once wrote, "knows what style of book he wants to write when he knows nothing else about it." What he should have added was that he knows what style he wants but lacks the faintest idea of how to create it.

Everything that rhymes is not poetry, and a lot that doesn't, is. Nor is everything that's mainly dialogue necessarily a play. Not all lies are fiction. Nonfiction is not that easy to write, either: Magazines, newspapers, and technical journals all have individual styles. The fact that we really managed to get something on paper doesn't mean anybody's going to want to read it, much less publish it.

There are now and always will be writers who can rise, rocketlike, from a completely uneducated background and, without any apparent acquaintanceship with grammar, syntax, or even spelling, produce a masterpiece, or at least something worth publishing. But be assured, they are a rarity, as out-of-the-ordinary as the child prodigy who picks up a violin at the age of three and, unrehearsed, plays a Mozart concerto. (Mozart himself was on a concert tour before the crowned heads of Europe when he was six and composed his first opera at eight.)

If we've reached the Golden Age without having displayed such remarkable talents, it's unlikely we'll suddenly develop them now, spontaneously. Therefore, an investigation of courses available for mature people who are beginning writers would seem to be in order—so much so that in the next chapter, I provide an introduction to the Wonderful World of *Adult*-Adult Education, particularly in the field of creative writing. You will be, as I was, astonished by the wide range of study opportunities available, often without cost, to men and women over fifty (up through the nineties) who are willing to go back to school.

But, right now, we're just considering the basic mechanics of writing, the nouns and verbs and the punctuation. If we were lucky enough to pass through the primary grades when the ability to diagram ("parse") sentences was still required, it may be all we'll need is a good handbook to recall what a dangling participle looks like. *The Elements of Style* by William Strunk and E. B. White, a wonderful and *little* manual, has served generations of writers. But if our rule of grammar was always limited to whether or not a thing "sounded all right," maybe some instruction in how sentences and paragraphs work would be a helpful prelude to setting up shop as a writer. The adult education courses I just mentioned specialize in helping people polish their English skills. It's hard to develop a style if you're not sure where the comma goes.

STEP THREE:
This brings us back to the two questions: Have we anything to say that will interest, amuse, or inform other people? What do we really *want* to write about?

It's also worth considering whether we're a one-article or one-book writer, interested only in finishing that manuscript we've been kicking around for half our lives, or whether we contem-

plate a brand new career and have five, ten, twenty or more manuscripts in mind. If we're going to go for the new career bit, then
we'd be wise to get into a course or study some how-to-write
books by people who've learned the hard way how to write copy
that sells. If we'll happily settle for the one-timer, then obviously
taking courses and starting a library of self-help literature is a
waste of money and effort. There must be an easier way to leave
one literary product to posterity; and there is.

We may write the story as best we can, type it up neatly and put
it in a stiff-cover binder, or have it professionally bound by a
bookbinder, if we want to give it a more permanent look. If we
want something still more elaborate, we can even have it printed.
Then, put it on the bookshelf alongside other books we treasure
and want to keep. There, our story will still be alive and well and,
above all, completed.

Meanwhile, let's do some self-examination and see if we have
the potential to become an ongoing writing machine. The best
way to do that is to make a list of things we already know we
want to say and of the tales we *want* to tell.

WRITE WHAT YOU CARE ABOUT

A good article or book, in my opinion, may be created only when
the writer has a strong, consuming interest in the subject, wants
to find out all about it, and then learns to communicate that interest to others. If we just visit a library, check over the best-seller
stacks, and come back with the great idea that there's a big market for books about sailing (a subject about which we have less interest and knowledge than a dog has about playing golf), we're going to produce a Grade A flop that won't get past the reception
desk of any publisher's office in the land. Some professional so-
called "hacks"—an undeservedly opprobrious term, since many
of them have writing skill and produce readable articles or books
about anything their sponsor or publisher wants to buy—are no-
name writers with prodigious outputs and no small incomes.
They work largely in, or on, the fringes of the advertising and public relations fields and, although much of their published work is
distributed free by satisfied sponsors, much of it is also found in
public libraries and schools and is very often welcomed by seek-

ers after specialized knowledge. In my days as a p.r. flack, I did a few such pieces myself. It was simply a case of producing 50,000 words or so about a company or product and getting paid for it without a professional editor in sight. It wasn't always easy: It was amazing how many company directors and vice-presidents in charge of nothing-in-particular fancied themselves as judges of good literature and practically re-wrote everything I wrote. I sometimes wonder how many of them have now become Senior Citizen writers and who, if anyone, is whacking *their* copy about and messing up their manuscripts.

Anyway, it's that kind of writing which, while it could bring you some satisfaction, is unlikely to fill your heart with delight. I gave it up when I retired, though I've been tempted by a few offers, and the subjects I write about must appeal, first of all, to me.

Follow that principle and it's possible to sell a manuscript to a publisher even when he, or she, has declared quite vehemently in advance that a book on such a subject would be of no possible interest to him and nobody would ever buy it.

How wrong can even a mighty publisher be? Take this as an example. Following is the Introduction from a book the publisher said he would never read:

> I was seventy-five!
>
> I enjoyed a quick breakfast, a walk in the sun, and a hearty lunch. I settled down for a midday nap, the privilege of the aging unemployed. Then—WHAM! It hit me. Any time now, it would be Black Friday for me or for my wife. One of us or both would say good-bye to all this and begin that last trek into the Great Beyond, with no hope of coming back. We didn't have so much as a road map.
>
> What had I done to prepare for the Big Day—next to my birthday, the most momentous day in my life? Precious little.
>
> I'd written a will of sorts, and that was it.
>
> What about the notary, lawyer, investment counsellor, trust company, insurance agent, medical doctor, hospital manager, undertaker, cemetery

owner, minister, priest, and the rest—all of whom
seemed to have a vested interest in my passing?
Not to mention that sturdy little band about to be
blasted from its foundations—the group referred to
by the statisticians as my "next of kin"? Shouldn't
I have done something about them?

I should, and now I have. In the process, I found
that dying isn't all that easy. It involves a lot of people and—like most other things in the real world—
masses of paper and dozens of decisions.

That's what this book is all about. It may save
you some time and trouble and make it easier for
those you leave behind. It will help you find out
who you are, who you should see, and what you
should be doing now—for, who knows, you may be
next.

Then it would be too late.

(from *Before You Die*, by Leonard L. Knott; John
Wiley and Sons, Toronto; Everest House, New
York)

Getting that little quote in here is what I call the "double wham-
my," or selling the same piece twice. It's something I'll ask you to
think about later—one man I know sold the same story (although
in different "treatments") more than thirty times and only gave
up when he became bored with it.

The point is, of course, if up to now it has escaped you, an author's consuming interest in a subject can make him or her write
about it so convincingly and so well that it will overcome even a
hard-boiled publisher's prejudice and get into print. I was interested in finding out how one dies *successfully*; the answers were
sufficiently interesting to make what I, and subsequently a publisher, thought would be an informative and entertaining book.

Another writer with no great interest in dying may be attracted
to some equally incongruous subject which will, if properly presented, captivate a bored publisher tiring of the endless parade of
sex, violence, and political intrigue. Marc Galant, a graphic designer who spends half his time in Europe and half in New York,
found such a subject in the lowly cow. He never forgot the dairy

farm in the village where he grew up, and he carried with him for years an attraction for cows which, he says, in contrast to bulls, have been ignored by writers, poets, and artists throughout history. In 1983, he set about remedying the situation and wrote a book, aptly called *The Cow Book*. It's all about (what else?) cows, and is said to be a very moo-ving tale. (Or should that be tail?) Knopf in New York bought it and immediately sold publishing rights to Sidgewick and Jackson in the U. K., Collins in Australia, Oerlag Saulander in Germany and Random House in Canada.

What would you or I have said if one day our neighbor had announced he was about to write a book about cows? Yet who knows? What interests you may one day fascinate the world.

MAKE UP A LITTLE (OR NOT SO LITTLE) LIST

In our process of taking stock, it might help to get us going (and remind us of how wide our interests really are) to make a list of things we might like to write about.

1. *Subjects in which we are interested*

It helps to start out with things we have some direct, firsthand experience of ourselves. Knowing your subject can be half the battle won before you begin.

(a) International intrigue, spies, undercover agents, and all that. But do we know anything about the spying racket other than what we've read in other writers' books? Perhaps, if we worked in the office of the CIA or are retired cops. If we toiled at more mundane pursuits, it's unlikely we'll ever be another John Le Carre or Len Deighton.

(b) Career stories. Many periodical and book publishers are interested in behind-the-scenes reports of take-over bids, fact pieces on how businesses work, why they succeed and why they fail, profiles of remarkable individuals. Who better than a retired executive or business consultant to give the "inside story" or adapt it for a novel or a series of short stories? Edward Mirvicka Jr. did it with his first book, *Battle Your Bank and Win*. Former chairman and chief executive officer of a national bank, he shows us how "to go up against your bank and come out the winner."

(c) Industrial disputes; battles between conglomerates, strikes, labor-management arguments, inter-company espionage. Here we're on safer ground: If we worked for a big company, we probably have some ready-made characters and some off-the-cuff plots. This might be a sound topic for a retired personnel relations person or labor union representative.

(d) Social or political causes. Almost everybody has a cause today, whether it's "stop the bomb" or finding homes for unwanted puppies. We haven't lost interest just because we're heading for retirement or have already arrived. Why not put our newly developed talents to work in support of the things we believe in, or against those we deplore? It beats demonstrating in the streets, particularly in cold or wet weather, and if we learn to write well and express ourselves forcefully, we can be much more persuasive. Remember Rachel Carson's *The Silent Spring*? Any number of publications would welcome the arrival of a literate older citizen who can "demonstrate" in print.

(e) High life, whether in New York, Paris, London, or Montreal. Scandalous doings in the glittering tall buildings. This could be duck soup for a former travel agent, hotel clerk, or fashion model; airline flight attendants have done it with remarkable flair.

(f) Love, romance, sex, and social behavior. Anyone can do this! Oh yeah!

(g) Ships and the sea. Adventure on water, or in the air. Good for retired sea dogs, former fishermen, astronauts, and white water enthusiasts. If you have a yacht, so much the better.

(h) Personalities. Politicians, war heroes, industry big-shots, crusaders, nurses, doctors, mad scientists. Call back your memories: Some interesting characters must have crossed your path whom you could fictionalize (so as not to get sued) and weave into a story, or write an article about.

(i) Horror! What gives you nightmares? Maybe you can scare somebody else with it, too.

(j) Any of the thousands of pastimes that attract people of any age, from stamp collecting to sky diving, just as long as it's something interesting to you and which you'd like to try to make interesting to others.

(k) How-tos. People are interested in articles telling them how to do almost anything. Remember jogging?

2. *Information sources*

Having chosen a subject, or subjects, we should go about establishing our sources: Where do we find our characters, descriptions, action experiences, particular examples, or statistics, etc.?

(a) Books we have read. A rather shaky source unless we have experiences or impressions of our own to add to it and to separate the sense from the nonsense. But books can provide us with much more than just the factual information they contain. To benefit from them fully, we must first learn how to read them— not just hop, skip, and jump through a book to find out how it comes out, and not just as researchers digging for facts. Thoughtful reading teaches us *how* to write, how to handle dialogue, how to organize our thoughts and our plots (by horrible example, perhaps). It helps keep us from writing difficult or ungrammatical sentences and makes us more aware of the variety of effective styles.

Not all successful writing is based on the writer's personal experiences. Many extremely talented mystery writers—Agatha Christie is probably the best example—never consorted with murderers or took part in a bank heist or a lineup. Stephen Crane's *The Red Badge of Courage* was based entirely on printed accounts, imagination, and insight into people. He had never fought in a battle, much less the actual Civil War Battle of Gettysburg which he so vividly described. And neither Clarence E. Mulford, who wrote all the Hopalong Cassidy books, nor Max Brand, author of *Destry Rides Again*, was ever a cowboy. It was all reading, research, and love of the era. And I'm reasonably sure that George Lucas, who wrote and directed *Star Wars*, never took a trip in a space ship. There are, after all, different kinds of knowing.

(b) Newspaper clippings. These are probably the greatest source for both fact and fiction writers. The daily newspaper is filled with reports, many of them just a few lines hidden on a back page, that give you plots, characters, excitement, tragedy, or comedy. Clippings are indispensable to the writer of topical articles or books. If you're on a special subject that needs a great deal of research, engaging a clipping service may be worthwhile. They're expensive but they'll bring you gobs of clippings you might otherwise never have seen. The clippings are no good, however, if you don't have some system of filing and preserving them, and tossing away the ones that are of no use.

There are dozens of companies throughout the United States and Canada providing clipping services. Some cover the continent, others are regional or strictly local. For information and addresses, try your local library, check advertising and business periodicals, or call and ask a local advertising agency or the advertising department of a big company. Charges are made at so much per clipping, with a monthly minimum of ten. When ordering a service, be very specific on what you want: If you ask for all clippings containing the word "epidemic," for instance, you'll be swamped—and bankrupt. Ask for references to diphtheria epidemics, or whatever.

(c) Authorities. People to whom we can write for information and, possibly, quotes. We may be longtime beekeeping enthusiasts but never as successful as the old lady in South Wabash who succeeded in crossing a northeastern honey bee with a southwestern stinger bee and produced a record crop of the sweet stuff. How she did it—if she'll tell us—could form an important part of our article or book. Similarly, if we're deep into a treatise about disarmament, it'd be nice to have a couple of quotes and from-the-horse's-mouth tips from someone who knew Bertrand Russell, one of the pilots who took that famous trip to Nagasaki, or a survivor who saw the plane coming. List possible sources at the outset (we may find them in the course of our reading) and get letters off to them quickly. Otherwise we'll be sitting there twiddling our thumbs, waiting to get started, or else we may be inundated with inserts and changes and corrections when we get around to the final draft and try to include what the replies told us. Also, if we're quoting either books or authorities, we should get permission in writing.

(d) People we know who could be helpful. This could be our friendly librarian, the local police chief or postman who often has interesting, gossipy stories to tell. It might be a local newspaper editor, family doctor, lawyer, undertaker, or garden expert next door. Any one of these might be a useful source, and we should keep their names on file. Another for-instance: Imagine we're writing a book about a family tragedy—wife beating, drinking, gambling—and we're stuck for a realistic description of what husbands and wives and third parties do or say. Our family doctor may have had some experiences; the postman may have been at the door at the crucial moment; the undertaker may recall a conversation with a bereaved spouse. We may have to change the names and the precise circumstances, but it's all grist for our mill.

(e) Our own memories. Call them up and make notes about those that are relevant. Here's one area where we have it all over Junior. No matter how smart he is, he can't remember what went on in 1940, say—twenty years before he was born. We can, because we were there. If we've kept our memories in a diary or a journal, we're jumps ahead; if we haven't, then we should try to call them up and record them as soon as we've chosen our subjects.

3. *Outline of article or book theme*

(a) If it's fiction, what is our basic idea for the plot? If it's nonfiction, what is the central idea, and how should it be developed?

(b) Who are the people involved, whether fictional or not? What are they like? What will it be important to tell the reader about them?

(c) Where does the piece happen? What important details do you want to mention to give the reader the feel of the place?

(d) Whether the piece is fiction or not, what main ideas do you want to get across to the reader? What are some good ways to *show* them, through particular examples, people, events?

TIME TO GET GOING!

That's our beginning. With charts like that in front of us, we're prepared to go to work. What eventually emerges will depend on our skill in translating all the resources we have assembled into readable prose (or verse). One thing for sure, we'll do a better job telling our story if we have first done a good job of preparing to tell it.

That's our gamble. When we look at the number of books, magazines, and newspapers that clutter bookstalls and newsstands, we cannot help wondering at the vast numbers of words that get into print, millions by people of whom we've never heard before. We can shudder at the thought of trying to compete in such an overcrowded world. Then, finally, we can come up smiling as we realize that, if they can do it, so can we. Authors whose names are found on every bookshelf didn't know they could write until they tried.

FIVE

Go Willingly to School

I grow old learning something new every day.

Solon (638-559 B.C.)

Old people learning isn't something new. Not only were the ancients of Rome and Athens teachers and philosophers, they were also scholars and students, eager to admit they didn't have all the answers. Every day and every night was a time for new discoveries as they learned to measure time and to map the heavens.

Yet today we still hear people say: "I don't need to learn how to write. I just have to make the decision to sit down and tell the story of my life. It's as easy as that."

Would that that were true. Certainly, anyone who can read can write, but there's a difference between being able to write and being able to write something that anyone else will read. The post office is flooded with first-class mail consisting of badly written manuscripts flowing back and forth between would-be writers and publishers. Included is an unbelievable number of "literary" outpourings that are straight gibberish, filled with mistakes in grammar and spelling, telling tales so incoherently that even long-suffering publishers' readers refuse to go beyond the first page.

Last fall, when I was spending a lovely afternoon in a little suburban bookshop autographing copies of my book *Writing for the Joy of It* (sell one copy and your afternoon's a success), I was approached by a woman whose age I wouldn't dare ask who wanted some advice about pursuing a literary career. "I have the titles for five short stories," she said, "but I've never written any of them because I don't know if they're any good or not. Do you think I should send the titles to a publisher and if he's interested, I could write the stories? I don't want to waste my time writing them if nobody would buy them."

I suggested maybe she should write one story, join a writing class and ask the teacher for an opinion. "Oh no," she said, "I wouldn't go to a writing class. I want these stories to be my very own and not have someone tell me how I should write them."

That, of course, is what they are likely to remain—her very own—not only unpublished but unwritten as well. She has yet to learn that writing stories or poems or essays that won't sell, revising them, tearing them up and starting all over again is part of the hard work of beginning to be a writer. And learning that after fifty or sixty is not always easy. But if you're not prepared to do it, then the best you can do is write what you like, as you like, for your own enjoyment and satisfaction and forget all about looking for a market. If writing itself gives you pleasure, that may be enough. Meanwhile, unless you've got something against money or have more of it than you're ever going to need, there's no harm in trying for the small change that's bouncing around out there in the marketplace. You may never ever reach for the top, but five, ten, fifteen or perhaps even fifty dollars now and then can do something for anybody's ego, help keep the home fires burning or pay the bar tab in that retirement village in southern California.

To write well enough to attract even an editor's passing interest, one must have some knowledge of the craft beyond being able to spell one's own name and address and add a ZIP Code, or having a host of reminiscences. Mark Twain once said: "Training is everything; the peach was once a bitter almond; cauliflower is nothing but a cabbage with a college education." A beginning writer, no matter what his or her age, is still a bitter almond or a cabbage if he or she has not had some kind of training. Since we who are Seniors in age are only Juniors in writing experience and in spirit, it behooves us to spend at least a fraction of our newfound time learning to become what we aspire to be.

Too old to go back to school and to start the learning process all over again? Balderdash! Lacydes, another one of those clever old Greeks, was studying geometry very late in life when someone asked him: "Is it then a time for you to be learning now?" Lacydes replied: "If it is not, when will it be?"

A MATTER OF MOTIVATION

"Many adults fear they can't learn as well as young students," says William Speigler, director of communications at C. W. Post College. "They think somehow their brain has slowed down and won't be able to cope with all that new information. Wrong! New research has shown that adults can learn as well and as quickly as young people, perhaps even faster, considering the fact that adults are frequently better motivated to learn than younger students." Take it from there, old-timers. We don't need to worry that our twenty-year-old grandson will think we're stupid if we land in the same class he's in. We may even inspire him to do a little better just to keep up.

Courses in creative writing are not confined to the rarefied halls of Harvard, Cornell, the University of Southern California and the like. Some of the most successful courses are given in out-of-the-way places. David McFadden, a professional writer, spent three years as a writing instructor at David Thompson University Center in Nelson, British Columbia. Writing for the Canadian book trade publication *Quill and Quire*, the north-of-the-border version of *Publishers Weekly*, McFadden took a special look at elderly students. "Some of my most gratifying moments came in working with two classes of old-timers," he wrote. "The classes were restricted to writers fifty and over, but most of the students were in their sixties and seventies with a few in their eighties. These old-timers hung on every word and were learning all the time; they remembered everything. They were for the most part retired people with vivid memories of the pioneer days ... and they knew exactly what they wanted: to write the stories of their lives, before it was too late.

"They were serious, but their seriousness was tempered with wisdom and self-knowledge. They weren't burdened with visions of literary glory; they just wanted to leave something behind when they died, something for their grandchildren, something for the government archives, a manuscript, modest immortality. We had a lot of fun in those classes, but there was also a lot of intensity. Every week everyone would bring in a new chapter or a revision of an old one, and sometimes there would be correspondence with publishers and editors to deal with collectively. And actual sales of stories and articles. ... When I left, most of them were well on their way to finishing their books; in fact, some had.

"In the context of a creative writing course, whether it involves kids in elementary school, young adults in college or university or retired people who want to write the story of their lives, it's important to zero in on such trivial concerns as spelling, punctuation and syntax. The old cliché is true; you simply can't write until you know all the rules."

Frank P. Thomas, who teaches an adult writing class at Ruskin, Florida, and whose book *How to Write the Story of Your Life* was published in 1984, has taught more than five hundred Seniors ranging in age from fifty to eighty-eight. "The Seniors I've taught," he told me, "are living proof that you can be creative at any age. Properly guided nonwriters turn out rich, nostalgic, entertaining, informative episodes dealing with their lives. Once they focus their minds on specific periods in their lives, they remember remarkably well. They are good listeners and when you offer writing techniques that will help them to produce a better quality of writing, they readily adjust to them. Some write with a pen, others with a typewriter, and a few have word processors."

Thomas's book is made up largely of examples of his pupils' work. A typical example is eighty-four-year-old Alex whose contribution was entitled "A Backward Look at a Fulfilled Life." "When he came into my class," Thomas says, "he was definitely a nonwriter. He was eager to learn, often interrupted me to ask questions. . . . In the presence of my wife and myself, he handed out his completed memoir. There were four generations of his family in the room at the time, little babies crawling around on the rug. Born in 1898, he's still going strong in 1985. When he left my class he said he wanted to go on beyond this first volume. He wanted to do a separate memoir about his foreign service experiences in many lands. The other day, he told me he'd completed it and taken it to a vanity press to publish."

FOR LOVE . . . OR MONEY?

Sure, I believe anyone who thinks he can write and gets pleasure out of doing it should go ahead and write for the joy of it—and to hell with teachers and editors and publishers and literary critics—and readers! And to hell, too, with dividends and royalties and checks. But if we who are over sixty-five and no longer on anybody's payroll want to do a little more than just have fun and could use a little extra income, then it's back to school, brothers and sisters. We're once more headed for the halls of academe—or, at least, the basement in the neighborhood church.

"Writing can't be taught" is an ancient shibboleth instantly acceptable to the lazy novice. It is given added currency by statements from contemporary best-selling authors that "creative writing courses destroy creativity" and that writing know-how somehow comes from inside, like a literary digestive burp. Perhaps they're right in some cases. Some English teachers do destroy their pupils' interest in literature, but many teachers have inspired their pupils to read good books and sometimes to write them. And why do so many successful writers take jobs as creative writing instructors in universities or become "writers in residence"? It can't be just for the money, which isn't that good.

People who want to paint don't hesitate to take art classes. Harry Lieberman took up painting when he was eighty, went to art class, and made a living at it when he was over 100. Photography schools are bustling with pupils, young and old, who want to learn how to take or make pictures. They can't all be crazy!

Pause for a moment while I tell you the story of late-starter Myrtle Brodsky.

A rich little English girl, born Myrtle Newton in 1893, Mrs. Brodsky grew up in comparative luxury. In her home were three maids and a gardener and until she was twenty-one she never even turned down her own bed. It wasn't popular for young ladies to be "educated" in those days, so her only academic achievement was to spend a year at finishing school in Germany. She was certainly never born to be a writer.

During World War I, Myrtle was a practical nurse with the Red Cross and a clerk in the postal censorship office. After the war, she married and moved to Canada, where she raised a family of five children. In the second World War, she was back in service, this time in the Canadian censorship bureau. At war's end, she went back to practical nursing and became a supervisor in an old-age home. Retiring in her seventies, she decided to go traveling and criss-crossed the United States by bus.

Then, at eighty, she made her great decision. Unable, because of her age, to get a job, tired of rattling about footloose and carefree, she decided to become a writer. First she went back to school and learned how to type. Then she began putting on paper articles based on exciting events from her own life. She began with a report of a coastal trip off Newfoundland and sold it to the *St. John's*

Telegram in the island capital. Since then, she has written dozens of travel articles for Canadian and American newspapers and magazines. In her nineties, she's still at it, specializing now in articles relating to growing old—a subject on which she says she is a natural authority.

I introduced myself to Myrtle Brodsky by mail after reading an article she had published in *The Writer* in the fall of 1983. The article urged older people to learn how to write so they could pass along their knowledge and their experiences to younger generations. She sent me a handwritten letter in reply: "I hope that this is legible," she wrote. "Muscular dystrophy prevents me from seeing what I write. Since my 80th year, I have been writing articles which were almost invariably published, on travel, special day pieces (Xmas, etc.), aging pieces, hearing aids, travel for seniors, etc. But it wasn't till my 90th year that I conceived the idea that my daily routine and method of coping would be of interest to others. I felt convinced that the aged all have a contribution to make by telling how they cope and the difficulties that beset all very old people—above all giving a picture of individual lifestyles which could perhaps be followed to advantage. I discovered the demand for aged lifestyle pieces by experiment and the resulting enthusiastic feedback.

"Yes, I slowed down about four years ago (at 86); for instance my travel pieces were all for travel by bus. One of the major bus companies gave me free passes for that purpose. Obviously my age precludes that now.

"All the freelancers I know began writing after the age of 65. My circle of acquaintances includes nobody 90 years or over, but I'm sure if you just listen to C.B.C.'s 'Over Ninety Club' on Sunday mornings that a mass of over-90 publication material is there, if only the owners of that material could be persuaded to submit it for publication."

At that point, Myrtle Brodsky had to close becase she was busy working on another magazine article with an imminent deadline.

Before we commence our new writing careers, let us admit to ourselves it's going to be work—maybe work we'll enjoy, maybe very hard work like Myrtle Brodsky at eighty learning to use a typewriter. Most of us have been out of school for a long time; we've lost the studying habit and must re-activate it. Some of us have been more fortunate and have been exposed to training courses at the office or factory or down on the farm, or have been professionals who had to keep up constantly with changing techniques and new discoveries. Good doctors never stop studying, because the practice of medicine is always changing and new medical products are always appearing on the market; engineers and architects are compelled to keep up with changes in materials, designs, and building codes; lawyers consult their libraries almost every day to look up cases and search for precedents. For men and women in those professions, going back to school is comparatively easy. (It's no surprise that many elderly writers turn out to be retired doctors, engineers, architects, or lawyers.)

LEARNING HOW TO LEARN
For those of us who served in more mundane occupations, it's a little more difficult. We need help just to learn how to learn. In several large cities, public libraries are conducting courses to teach Senior Citizens how to use the library, a practice about which many of them, apparently, knew very little. A vocational guidance session or aptitude test may be helpful—something that will tell us if we're really suited for what we are about to undertake. (I say this with some reservations because when I was thirty-six, my aptitude tester told me that the one thing I was not suited for was to become a writer. Had I followed his advice, I wouldn't have written this book and would have missed a lifetime of fun.) Talks with English teachers, having them read a sampling of what we've already written, might be more useful.

Once tested and found either qualified or wanting, we can decide, if we're still interested, what kind of course or courses we want to take, under what circumstances and at what cost, and how to go about finding them.

Let's approach this whole subject of post-retirement learning calmly and without being pushed too rapidly one way or another. We haven't got all that time to waste. An old friend of mine, still a successful practicing surgeon at eighty-five, took an arts degree along with me back in the twenties. Then he decided to be a farmer and went to agricultural college for three years. He gave up the farming idea when he found he was allergic to cows, alfalfa, and heavy labor and decided to settle for dentistry. Before taking his final lesson in how to extract a molar, he switched to medicine, took four years at medical school, two years post-graduate school in London, and one year interning. He became a specialist in certain surgical operations, opened a clinic of his own in New York State, and is there today as chief surgeon. Learning time: twenty-two years. A bit much for someone starting at fifty or over.

So, let's be sure writing is what we want; then, what kind of writing. If fiction is on our mind, what do we do: finish the old story or start a brand new one? Whichever choice we make, let's get it on paper the best way we can. If we read it over and think, "That's great stuff, better than most of the junk printed today," let's go for an outside *professional* opinion. Not our sister's, nor Uncle Joseph's, the mining engineer's, nor even cousin Effie's, who's in the advertising business. And that well-known writer who lives just down the street and has lunch every Wednesday at the Hot Spot cafeteria isn't going to welcome a visit from us with a request: "Would you mind reading this and telling me if it's any good?" He's not an editor or a writing consultant; he hates reading other people's manuscripts and, anyway, he doesn't know what makes an article or a book saleable. If he did, he'd be one of the few millionaire writers and wouldn't be eating in a cafeteria.

GETTING A SECOND OPINION

Where do we find *professional* opinions? The closest, quickest, but not necessarily the surest is from an editor whose business is buying the kind of thing we're hoping to sell. So, let's go looking for an editor. First we check *Writer's Market* or *Literary Market Place*, the two annual listings of book and periodical publishers and editors. Then we go through a few recent copies of *Writer's Digest* or *The Writer*, two monthly magazines that are published solely in the interests of people like us who are interested in both writing and selling. Available in most public libraries (subscriptions are suggested if we intend to continue writing), these two publications regularly carry reports from editors and publishers about their current requirements, what they are paying, and whether or not we get cash in advance or wait for publication. They also carry announcements about publications or book publishers that have gone belly-up or are delinquent in making payments. That's very useful information to have in these perilous times in the book and magazine trades.

Following this diligent search, which should be conducted with great care so that the manuscript we eventually mail will reach its most likely market, we make sure our copy is clean-typed, properly identified as to source and then sent off, with a self-addressed stamped envelope enclosed, to the lucky editor who is about to let us know what a great writer we are. The worst that will happen is that the manuscript will come back with a printed rejection slip that tells us absolutely nothing except that the editor doesn't want it; the best is a letter from an editor, in his own envelope, not ours, saying he or she loves our story, will be delighted to publish it, and will send us a check or a contract forthwith. (We should frame it, in case we never get another.)

In between best and worst is the letter we were really looking for in the first place; not a sale, but an encouraging or discouraging word. We'll have one reasonably dependable professional opinion on the viability of our decision to become a writer. But just *one*. We need neither go cloud-floating nor sink into despair; all we have is a guidepost to our future, something to work on.

Editors and publishers are not omniscient. They make mistakes, and we don't need to take one editor's opinion as the Gospel according to St. John—except, of course, the one that came along with the check. His or her opinion we can accept as having some credibility and we can proceed merrily towards the creation of our next masterpiece. We are, after all, the answer to hungry readers' prayers.

We may, of course, make another interesting discovery. Our first story sold because we were so wrapped up in it, knew the subject so well, that it became *the one story we had to tell*. The success story we may never repeat. We don't have our initial interest and enthusiasm, and we have never been trained to write consistently. The words just won't flow. Yes, we have shown we have talent, but we're lacking in skill, so we better hustle off to school.

The editor who sends us a no-comment rejection slip need not be taken as a final arbiter. He or she may have had a bad morning; he may have been summoned to a meeting and simply dumped all unread or half-read manuscripts into an out-basket. Or he may have instructions from Big Brother upstairs that the shop's overloaded with manuscripts, can't handle any more, and get rid of the logjam. Nothing in the printed slip tells us any of that. Stuff it away in the "file and forget" folder and send it off to choice number two.

If the result is the same—no word, just rejection—we should ponder, take a second look at the manuscript, maybe make a few changes, then send it out one time more. For these trying-to-get-an-editorial-opinion efforts, three times is out and we must consider seeking a judgment from someone who is not interested in buying anything, not even a first edition of the Dead Sea Scrolls, but who makes a business or profession out of telling people who write what's good or bad about their writing.

The editor who sent us an in-between rejection letter should be taken very seriously. He or she may turn out to be our very best friend. The very fact that he took the time to discuss our story at all indicates that he saw possibilities in it, that somewhere between the lines there was a glimmer; that next time, if some corrections, alterations, and revisions were made, our story might make it. We can do one of two things: follow that advice we have received for nothing and hope the revised manuscript will live up to the editor's professed expectations, or take the manuscript and letter to a professional teacher and get help in making the changes.

We now face the problem of finding the professional help. We go back to school and we look for a class and a teacher, or teachers, who we think can *one,* give us a frank and helpful opinion and, *two,* provide the kind of instruction or guidance that will help us sell what is otherwise an unsaleable manuscript—and, more importantly, more manuscripts in the future.

A SHORT COURSE ON SCHOOLS

There are all sorts of people and institutions out there eager and willing to take our money. Some of them promise that if we listen to their counsel and follow their instructions we will become not only famous but rich. The credibility of those promises we must assess for ourselves. Obviously, everyone who takes a writing course is not going to be either. Some will attend every class, make notes at every lecture, read all the prescribed texts, write all the required compositions and emerge quite incapable of writing as much as a single page of comprehensible prose. Just as a word processor cannot make us better writers but can help us produce neater manuscripts, a writing instructor can only help us organize our ideas and improve our language. If we are not story-tellers to begin with and do not have within us the imaginative and descriptive powers to stir our readers, writing instructors can rarely perform miracles and make us popular writers. Of one thing only may we be reasonably sure: We will probably write better, more coherently, more effectively if we are properly trained than we did before. And that's not all bad.

In the same writers' publications that gave us the names of editors and publishers there are advertisements for correspondence schools, literary agents, and consultants who will tell us, for a fee, whether we have the makings of authorship or should stick to truck driving or amateur gardening. Among these advertisers are some who are so anxious to help us in our quest they offer to read our manuscripts free of charge, make an honest appraisal and tell us whether or not we should then hire them to teach us to do better. Naturally, these appeals are not 100 percent objective; behind them lurks the profit motive which tells their sponsors that a positive answer to our enquiry will lead to a further, profitable (for them) relationship; a negative response will terminate it.

We can ask the advertiser to send us the names and addresses of some of his pupils from whom we might obtain an evaluation of his "product"; or we might ask him for the names of graduates or former pupils who have become even moderately successful as writers. This would give us names we could check at our public libraries, either on the shelves, in the catalogues, or in *Books in Print*, a continuing series of volumes containing the names of all books that are still in print. Reassuring letters from former pupils might persuade us to enroll. As a further precaution we could request an opinion from the National Writers' Union of Canada in Canada). While both organizations are set up to assist their members, they are also concerned about unethical practices in the writing business and will probably warn unsuspecting, nonmember authors about writing-teacher sharks.

Before getting into the subject of courses specially designed for Seniors, let's consider the field open to anyone, regardless of age. Those of us who live in big cities are literally surrounded by learning opportunities ranging from English courses in high schools and junior colleges to creative writing courses in universities. Many teachers who have taught both adult and college-age classes suggest that older students do better when they are not segregated and are members of regular undergraduate classes. They suggest we'd do well to enroll in a university or high school class and go back to school along with our grandchildren. We should, however, be more selective than most Juniors are likely to be, choosing not the "soft" course that will lead to easy examinations but the course that will do us the most good in our future endeavors. A pre-enrollment interview with the course director or a career adviser, with a request for an assessment of our work, could protect us from joining a class that has very little to offer and will be a waste of our time. And a careful study of the subjects being taught and the credentials of the instructors could prevent an aspiring old-age historian from spending an entire semester in a classroom discussing nuclear energy or scripting for television.

Directories listing university courses open to Seniors are available and it is noted that in many cases tuition for students over sixty-five is very often waived or discounted.

Outside the formal educational institutions, there are in most cities and many smaller towns private organizations set up to conduct adult education. Their classes are usually held at night; teachers, if not volunteers, are semi-professionals and the "spice" is provided by visiting "name" lecturers who may be big guns in the writing field but complete flops as instructors. We should accept them as entertainers and be grateful for the opportunity to glimpse the literary great. Many of these courses are given in community halls, YMCA's, churches and synagogues. Throughout the year, professional, amateur, and beginning writers, and people who just enjoy seeing writing folk in the flesh are invited to seminars and workshops, some of them of dubious value, except as entertainment.

To add to our fun, and to make sure that we enjoy writing as a second career, we are also invited to attend summer holiday workshops held on college campuses and at resorts. There, formal education and summer relaxation combine and one may have just as good a time as on one of those literary bus tours in Old England or barge cruises in the French canals with visits to old chateaus. Senior Citizens, whether writers or just people who enjoy meeting, mingling and hero-worshipping with them, are welcomed at these outdoor seminars. Particulars may be secured from the English departments of most universities; a list of workshops is published every year in *Writer's Digest*.

OTHER AVENUES OF LEARNING

Educating the older generation, with special courses designed for Seniors, is the "in" thing in the eighties and promises to be even more so in the nineties and on into the twenty-first century as the number of Senior Citizens continues to grow. Most of these courses are devised to instruct old people in the art of growing even older; the study of gerontology is the major subject. But diligent searching will drag up a writing course. Probably the most extensive educational program for older Americans is the one offered by the Institute of Lifetime Learning, a service of the National Retired Teachers' Association which is, in turn, an affiliate of the American Association of Retired Persons. Unfortunately, their official literature reveals very little interest in creative writing as a subject suitable for Seniors, and inquiries I made about classes for men and women who might aspire to be writers stirred very little enthusiasm—leading me to suspect, probably incorrectly, that most of the retired teachers were scientists or mathematicians. But this organization is strongly dedicated to getting us oldsters out of our rocking chairs and into the classrooms, so an avalanche of letters from would-be writers might stimulate action.

If you're interested, the organization issues a printed program guide to its whole series under the title *Learning Opportunities for Older Persons*. Copies are available from 1909 K Street NW, Washington DC 20049.

Another informative and useful publication for those looking for classes for the elderly is *Learning Times*, a tabloid newspaper for adult learners. "Americans," according to a *Learning Times* editorial by Ronald Gross, author of *The Lifelong Learner*, "are suddenly discovering a new way to enrich their lives and to reach for new goals. It goes by various names and takes different forms: continuing education, adult education, lifelong learning, part-time study, television courses, returning to college either in pursuit of a degree or just to learn more about something of interest.

"One out of five adults is enrolled in some form of education or training," Gross reports. That means about five million upper-age students.

Learning opportunities, including everything from animal husbandry to xylophone playing, are available in colleges and universities, in community centers and local schools, in libraries, museums and in housing projects. Some are free; others are not.

Learning Times points out that "many communities have counseling centers that can help you find out what you want and assist you in discovering your own interests, abilities, and special talents." (Perhaps there's a fiction-writing expert sitting there with the opinion and advice we're looking for!) The Regional Counselling Center of Southeastern Connecticut is an example: "We help adults who come to us for advice to go through a three-pronged process," reports Peg Atherton, director. "If you came to us for counseling first, I would help you with value clarification, finding out where your real interests lie. Second, I would ask you to think about and define your career goals, broad or narrow. Third, I would help you decide what education you need to meet your goals." What more could a new writer ask?

The Connecticut Center is but one of many; for a national list write: National Center for Educational Brokering, 2211 Connecticut Avenue NW, Washington DC 20036. For copies of *Learning Times*, write College Board, Publication Orders, Box 2815, Princeton, New Jersey 08541.

My files are bulging with letters and pamphlets and folders about senior education opportunities. Here are just a few items, selected at random.

Valencia Community College, Open Campus, Orlando, Florida, has a Creative Writing Workshop offering classes in the basics of creative writing skills, including style, short stories, novels, magazine and newspaper features and research. Commencing in September, courses are given at deMay St. Cloud High School, Indiana Avenue, St. Cloud, and Fowler West Campus, 1800 S. Kirkman Road, Orlando. Courses are also offered in various subjects throughout Orange and Osceola counties, Florida, in community and senior centers, retirement and adult congregate living facilities, churches, nursing homes and adult day care centers. There is no registration fee for students fifty-five and over. To have a creative writing course in one of these centers, interest in attending would have to be expressed by at least fifteen individuals.

For eager beaver Seniors who can't wait to get their fingers on a word processor and other high tech instruments, Louisiana Tech is offering free courses in computers for retired persons. Introductions are provided to using micro-computers (personal computers), word processors, and accounting programs. Senior Citizen rates are available for campus housing and food services during June, July, and August. For more information, write to Dr. Charles Bolz, Louisiana Tech University, Box 7923, Ruston, LA 71272.

In Canada, most provincial universities and colleges schedule special courses for Seniors. An example is the 1985 program at McGill University's Center for Continuing Education. The program's overall theme is "Keeping Up with Change." At least one of the courses deals with computers. You can get information on the program from McGill University Center for Continuing Education, Redpath Library Building, 3461 McTavish Street, Montreal, P. Q. H3A 1Y1.

The Northeastern Senior Seminar Program at Skidmore College (about which we'll talk more later) offered such a course for one week in 1981. Sixty-five enrolled but only half attended and the experiment was not repeated. Future classes would depend on a sincere indication of interest.

There's been a recent development in the "old folks" educational circuit that could help those of us who would like to find classes attended by our peers. It's the Learning Network. A data base is used to create a learning exchange between people with skills and others who want to learn those same skills. This type of activity operates in many settings: urban, rural, school-based, library-based, and independently, under a wide variety of names. Groups are set up under such titles as Learning Connection,

Learning Network, Human Resources File, Resource Center, People Index, Neighborhood Talent and Resource Registry, Information Exchange, and Skills Bank. One of the best known is the Learning Exchange in Evanston, Illinois, and individuals interested in exchanging, whether their skills as writers or their desire to acquire those skills, should write to the Director of National Programs, The Learning Exchange, P.O. Box 920, Evanston, IL 60204. The Exchange also publishes a newsletter, *Interchange.*

The National Community Education Clearinghouse Incorporated, 6011 Executive Boulevard, Rockville, MD 20852, has information about community education opportunities and will also identify persons in different areas who can speak about community education projects involving older persons.

Two other publications recommended by the Institute of Lifetime Learning to help us find courses are: The *Education Directory* published each year by the National Center for Educational Statistics, available in most libraries and *Alternatives for Later Life and Learning,* listing some programs designed especially for older persons and offered at state colleges and universities. Copies of the latter are available from the American Association of State Colleges and Universities, Suite 700, 1 Dupont Circle, Washington, DC 20036.

In New York City, Fordham University conducts a special program for Seniors at its Lincoln Center campus, known as the "College at Sixty." Its activities were featured in a CBS-TV documentary called "Don't Ever Grow Old if You Can Help It," and quoted Vic Miles: "The College at Sixty program is one of the most imaginative and constructive alternatives to roleless retirement that has come to my attention." With all that, there must be a place in there somewhere for elderly writers. Classes are held once a week, for two hours, at midday.

And finally, for Seniors who like fun as well as work but don't feel quite up to frolicking with their Juniors at seminars such as the Vermont Bread Loaf Writers' Conference, there is the imaginative and fun-filled Elderhostel program conducted by Skidmore College and known officially as the Northeastern Senior Seminar. Nine colleges and universities in the United States and Canada cooperate in this program and participants, all sixty or over, spend a week or more at one of their campuses, living as the carefree students they once used to be. Not all the colleges offer the same courses, and programs vary from year to year; it's necessary to select a program well in advance. In 1983, for instance, Bard College, on the east bank of the Hudson River, some 90 miles north of New York City, was the only one appealing to Senior writers and it offered a course on "Writing Your Memoirs" which it described as follows: "The central work of this workshop is the participant's own writing along with the articulation, both private and shared, of response to it. Readings will be undertaken from contemporary and traditional works towards development of introspective and effective forms and a balance between vision and craftsmanship."

Whoever knew that writing one's memoirs could be so complicated!

LEARNING AT HOME

If we can't find a course that suits us, or don't want to leave home to attend one, we may either sign up for a correspondence course or do what hundreds have done before us—teach ourselves with the aid of "textbooks" written for our benefit by some of the best writing teachers there are—men and women who know how to write and to sell and have proved it by doing it.

There's no problem in filling half a dozen bookshelves with "how-to" books about writing; there's one to fit every purpose, style, or mood. From the hundreds on sale, from a dozen different publishers, I have selected about two dozen, with the help of fellow writers, since not even I could have read them all. Their titles, authors, and publishers are included in the Bibliography at the end of *this* book—the only one of the lot that I can absolutely and unreservedly recommend.

If you'd like to know more about correspondence schools, here are a few you might consider: Christian Writer' Guild, 260 Fern Lane, Hume, CA 93628; Famous Writers School, 17 Riverside Ave., Westport, CT 06880; The Institute of Children's Literature, Redding Ridge, CT 06876; National Writers Club, Suite 620, 1450 S. Havana, Aurora, CO 80012; Writer's Digest School, 9933 Alliance Road, Cincinnati, OH 45242.

All of these are reputable and have been in business for years and years. If you decide to register, you'll be put in contact with an experienced instructor who will give and evaluate assignments and provide you with detailed commentaries on the strengths and weaknesses of your writing. Some have courses in most phases of writing; others are more specialized. Choose those that are most appropriate to your interests and drop them a note requesting descriptive literature.

There you have it: a one-man summary of back-to-school opportunities for those who are learning to write after fifty. If you still think that the whole exercise is silly for mature people who should have something better to do with their time, pay heed to the words of Dr. Perry Gresham, educator, lecturer, retired business executive and author of a book for Senior Citizens called *Wings as Eagles:* "Those who have vision and expectancy and a spirit of creative adventure, go on to the happiest and best years of their lives."

Life for them truly begins at sixty—or seventy—or seventy-five. Or, as the Jewish mother said to the school principal whom she visited to complain that her son had received only 97 in his examinations: "What's the matter, there isn't any 100?"

SIX

Memories: Money in the Bank

Memory is the diary that we all carry about with us.

Oscar Wilde—*The Importance of Being Earnest*

In this one respect, we who are over fifty are richer than all our Juniors. Should they try to write about the past, they must depend upon hearsay, other people's books, or other people's research. We can write about what we know, what we saw or heard or experienced. There's no satisfactory substitute for having been there. If half the history books are wrong, it's likely because they were written by writers who had to depend upon what somebody else told them, either verbally or in books or songs, or rely on their own imaginations, which are not necessarily noted for accuracy.

Milton suggested that as we grow old, if we just sit and think, "Time will run back and fetch the age of gold." Prettily expressed but not quite literally true! A lot more than just sitting and thinking is required to transform memories into gold. But it is a fact that a well-remembered yesterday may contribute generously to a richer tomorrow, if we make the proper efforts.

Nostalgia is popular as we near the end of the twentieth century. While millions of anxious people peer into the future, other millions as eagerly examine the past. Those who can remember the century's beginnings or middle years have at firsthand a product that many editors and readers find increasingly beguiling. During our lifetimes we, personally, pioneered in using the telephone, listening to radio, and watching television. We were the first generation to ride about in automobiles, fly in airplanes, and watch the astronauts take off for the moon. We, or our neighbors, fought in two world wars, mourned the collapse of the League of Nations, and watched with hope the birth of a new organization for world peace. We've lived through hundreds of fads— from the turkey trot to the Beatles, from bustles to mini-skirts to jeans, from mah-jongg to video games and Trivial Pursuit.

If we grew up on farms or spent our lives there, we saw the

plough horse give way to the combine and witnessed acres of land being transformed from deserts to fields and fruit orchards. Meanwhile, small towns became big cities and big cities gave us new landmarks with the first skyscrapers, then high-rises, sub-ways, and shopping plazas, opera houses, and museums. Metro-polises undreamed of when we were very young now dot the land-scape from coast to coast.

LETTING OUR MEMORIES SOAR

What a bagful of memories we have! We should not waste them on oft-repeated, boring dinner table tales or bury them as thinly disguised preachments to our grandchildren. Let's find ways to let them soar, to reach the eyes and ears of a more receptive out-side world that knows us not and will therefore be more willing to accept our reminiscences and literary flashbacks as genuine ar-ticles, worth possibly a small price of admission. With always-in-the-family flashbacks, familiarity may breed yawns. We need a wider audience.

We are fortunate if we are among those who kept diaries or jour-nals, not just the kind Oscar Wilde refers to as occupying our minds, but real diaries and journals we can look at and pick up and read. Unaided memories sometimes play strange tricks, or create doubts and hesitations that inhibit us when we approach a typewriter and seek to put them on paper. Can I, who cannot re-member the name of my closest neighbor or how much I paid for a basket of tomatoes at the supermarket, be sure that what I re-member about a night in August, 1923 is true? I'm told that old people are often unable to recall what happened the day before but can describe with complete accuracy a meeting that took place fifty years ago. But can we be sure? A diary or journal would be invaluable to us now, guaranteeing accuracy and allowing us to write with confidence knowing that we could never be contra-dicted.

Alas, too many of us are like the hero in Irwin Shaw's novel *Bury the Dead* who, as he approached the end of life, remarked: "There are too many books I haven't read, too many places I haven't seen and too many memories I haven't kept long enough." If only our Juniors could become as wisely young as we have become wisely old, what advantages they would have in their later years. They still have time to read the books, visit the places, and preserve the memories so that when they are over fifty they may be prepared to exploit their past. We can only draw upon the memories we have and hope they are enough to enable us to create the kind of manuscripts that benevolent editors will want to buy and gentle readers will want to read.

MEMOIRS—NOT FOR THE MUNDANE

When one thinks of writing about the past, one's first thoughts turn to a book of memoirs or an autobiography. I'm sorry to have to report that these should be at the bottom of our lists—*unless* (1) we are very famous or infamous, and a world of readers is champing at the bit waiting to learn how we became so and what fascinating adventures or scandals we engaged in en route; or (2) we were attached to some famous or infamous person or persons and through telling our own story are really revealing facts or fancies about theirs; or (3) we witnessed or participated in some famous or infamous event (like a dash to the Pole or the development of the atom bomb) and our lives are incidental to the recitation of the event itself; or, finally, (4) we are content to leave our projects, typewritten, photocopied, or self-published for the edification of our families, friends, and particularly our heirs as a reminder that we once walked upon this earth and had memories and tales to tell.

There is one other exception to the general rule that might make a book of memoirs acceptable to a publisher even if the market for it appears relatively small. A technical-type biography relating our experiences in a specified industry, profession, or science would have some potential, though it might consist very largely of descriptions of our contacts with other careerists better known than ourselves. *Behind the Scenes in Television*, a record of fifty years on the boob tube, could draw a respectable audience of fans though they might not be the least bit interested in us, or even know who we were.

Let's stay for another moment with that most popular of all subjects for first-time Senior writers—ourselves. As both teachers McFadden and Thomas attest, by far the great majority of over-fifty students take their courses in order to learn how to write the story of their lives. They think not of commercial publication, though teacher encouragement and discovery of a latent talent may lead them there eventually. What they want to do most is leave their descendants a living document from unique and irreplaceable sources. Generations to come, they hope, will cherish the chance to look back and examine their roots.

It was recognition of this consuming interest among his older students that prompted Frank Thomas to publish *How to Write the Story of Your Life*. And it was a passage from that book quoting Russell Baker, author of *Growing Up*, that prompted me to suggest we go a stage farther and include our families in our little histories. "We all come from the past," Baker wrote, "and children ought to know what it was that went into their making, to know that life is a braided cord of humanity stretching up from time long gone, and that it cannot be defined by the span of a single journey from diaper to shroud." So surely we should be prepared to tell little Mary or little Johnny, who will be born in the new twenty-first century, who some of their ancestors were, including their great-great aunts and uncles and not just us.

DELINEATING YOUR ROOTS

Writing a family history, of course, can become a staggering undertaking—one's ancestors increase in number alarmingly, generation by generation. When the world decided in 1985 to celebrate the three hundredth anniversary of the birth of Johann Sebastian Bach, researchers, somewhat to their dismay, traced more than three hundred descendants of the famous composer, all bearing the surname Bach. These represented male descendants through direct male lines only; had female descendants, or male or female offspring of females been included, there would have been enough members of the Bach family alive to populate a fair-sized city.

It's obvious that in undertaking to write our family histories, we must impose very strict limitations or we'll quickly find ourselves in a seemingly endless genealogical morass.

Every English-speaking person, it is said, and thousands of those who speak French and German, including natives of former colonies, can trace their ancestry back to an English king, or an English highwayman, pirate, or whiskey smuggler. In effect, whether or not we love our neighbor, there is a very distinct possibility that somewhere back in the reaches of time, we have a common ancestor.

Where do we begin? Unless we intend to spend the rest of our lives in some primordial maze, we'll select the branch of the family to which we are immediately attached and never stray farther away than our uncles and aunts and cousins who share our grandparents or great-grandparents. For simplicity's sake, rather than because of any male chauvinism, when we get into the greats and the great-greats and the great-great-greats, we'd better stick to those who bear the family name and continue in direct line as far back as we can go. There are exceptions, of course. One or more remarkable woman may have preceded us in the family and cause us to direct our research into the female side. No one would willingly dismiss from their family record a reference to a Sarah Bernhardt or a Harriet Beecher Stowe.

However diligent we may be in seeking and preserving family records, we will still benefit by seeking help from relatives. This in itself may lead us to some interesting and enriching experiences. While using one relative to help find another, we may reach family members we never knew existed or knew only through remembered conversations with our parents or grandparents many years ago.

Frank Thomas suggests that we begin by approaching relatives we know, particularly older ones, whose memories we may tap. We should go armed with tape recorders or notebooks, be prepared to let garrulous aunts and uncles wander, and encourage timid or noncooperative ones to speak up.

After these first encounters, we might prepare a questionnaire to send to out-of-town relatives asking them for information about their immediate family histories, personal recollections, and any facts they may have about our common ancestors. A friend who is seriously attempting to get his family history on paper tells me he is having a dreadful time even getting answers to his queries. Most of his relatives just aren't interested. That's just one of the hazards of history writing, I tell him, and he perseveres; and gradually, a quite comprehensive family record is taking shape.

Not one in a million—or fewer: Say, not more than half a dozen in 200 million—are prepared to go as far as Alex Haley did when he blazed a trail backwards to his ancestral village in Africa and produced the best-selling chronicle *Roots*. But there are many ways in which less energetic or ambitious folk can satisfy the urge to know what they are and pass that information on to their descendants. Church records, files of civic registry offices, old telephone directories and old newspaper files, and copies of *Who's Who* are all open to family researchers and may serve as guides to help them in their search.

TELLING IT LIKE IT WAS

Fortunately, books of memoirs are not the only medium available to memory-writers. Even the youngest of our Juniors today—and perhaps they more than anyone else—are interested in knowing something about the world as it was B.T. (Before Television) or even B.C. (Before Computers). And they're not to be satisfied with dull history texts overloaded with dates. John Matthews, a twenty-three-year-old university student from Toronto, is headed for a career in engineering or science: He's not quite sure which. Either way, he spends half his days with computers and other electronice devices, the rest of the time with books of calculus and lectures on stress and strain. When he gets a few moments' leisure time he likes to read sea stories—books or articles about wooden ships and iron men or about the first days of steam. He devours Joseph Conrad, knows by heart the adventures of Captain Hornblower. His favorite is *Moby Dick*. He prefers tall ships to space ships, yet he is a man of the future.

Stories about the Big Bands are often gobbled up by second and third generation readers behind us. They'd grab for an article on Benny Goodman by an observer who was there and has a knowledge of what Big Band music was all about. We lived through the Jazz age and were familiar with Paul Whiteman and Tommy Dorsey and Cab Calloway and the host of performers who surrounded them—Eddie Cantor, Kate Smith, and Dennis Day. Some of us even danced to Alexander's Ragtime Band.

Those performers are all on records—special packages advertised in the Senior Citizen magazines—but the youngsters want more than records. They want the feel of what it was like to be there. They can get that only from us. Those of us who can master a way of describing life in the twenties or thirties in short stories, poetry, or prose will find a young audience as eager as our peers to catch an authentic glimpse of the past.

We tend to take our past for granted, except to grumble about the changes that have taken place along our way. We never did anything exciting. We were stay-at-homes, nose-to-the-grindstone people fully occupied with paying bills and raising children. We forget that our past is almost a never-never land for even middle agers who never heard of the bunny hug, bobbed hair, the shimmy, Happy Hooligan, or cars with right-hand drives.

I tried an autobiography once but, being neither famous nor infamous enough, I couldn't find a publisher who'd buy it. The best I could do was get a glimmer of interest from an editor who spotted a chapter headed *Waltztime in Winnipeg*, all about my birthplace in the days before World War I. Lift that one out, he said, and he'd consider buying it as an article. What caught his eye was a paragraph in which I told about my grandmother and me sitting on the verandah and counting the automobiles driving by. One Sunday afternoon, we counted twenty-three cars; that many go by in a minute today. (I'm not too sure Grandma would have considered that to be an improvement; for one thing, it made it more difficult to cross the street.)

So, nostalgia is one of the most saleable commodities we've got, and newspapers, magazines, specialized trade and hobby or recreational publications are all in the market for it. We can exploit it by working these memories of ours to the limit, picking a period, an event, or an experience that we remember and making it the subject of our writing project. It could be a setting for a short story: "Henry and Madeleine were ardent canoeists. Sometimes he'd paddle and she'd recline lazily in the bow, her fingers trailing in the water. Other times, she'd take the paddle and he'd strum away on his ukelele. They didn't notice the storm coming up or remember the thirty foot dam that was just ahead. . . ." It could provide the backdrop for a complete novel, something like Booth Tarkington's *Seventeen*, with a little touch of sophistication, of course, but nevertheless vintage 1920. Perhaps that's where we might resurrect our unfinished story that we didn't have time for in the forties or fifties.

More likely, our memory piece will be more suitable for the Sunday supplements. There are more than 1,800 daily newspapers in the United States, 100 in Canada; many of them publish special weekend editions or separate Sunday editions that buy free-lance material. Or a popular magazine with a local orientation might be interested. Rarely, unless we are authorities on literature, drama, the dance, or some other esoteric activity, will we find a market in the so-called quality press. It's there, but it's harder to reach.

WRITING FOR THE NOSTALGIA MARKET

The important thing is that we know who or what we are writing for and then capture and set down on paper the atmosphere, the feeling, and the excitement of our time in a manner and form acceptable to today's rock generation. Doing that is not only going to put *our* memories to work but may demand help from the memories of our relatives and friends, or the odd trip to a library or the school or university we used to attend. We'll haul out the old diaries, journals, letters, and any scraps of paper we can scrounge from the past, examine old school yearbooks, newspaper clippings, and other people's letters and records we've gathered over the years. Most of us have photo albums, or dresser drawers filled with old faded prints, which serve to stir our memories and remind us of what the people we knew looked like when we were younger. They'll also help us recall happenings—sometimes sad and sometimes merry. A good time to rescue these nostalgic documents is when, after retirement, we move from a house to an apartment, from the cold north to the warm south or to some other city to be near the children. If we're lazy, papers and files go to the trash by the barrel-load; if we're wise and want to write, we'll hang on to all the bits and pieces and guard them with our lives.

Assembling all this "attic" material, getting it in some kind of order and supplementing it with notes taken at the library or school or from family conversations, will give us a "memory journal" that we can draw upon as we settle down to work. For starters, and this may surprise you, there's an editor somewhere trying to turn out an interesting magazine for the shoe trade or the grocery business whose day would be made if an article titled "No One Had Ever Heard of Rubber Heels," or "My Best Seller was Sarsaparilla by the Barrel," came in over the transom.

We don't want to write "shop," however, so we'll begin with a locale: town or city where we lived; next, the time: the 1920s (or 1930s). We'll enter in our memory journal everything we remember, or have in our documentary file, about our town at that time: who the neighbors were and who was mayor—with anecdotes, if any; what Main Street was like, who ran the general store—(don't forget the little money carriages that ran overhead from the counter to the cash desk upstairs). What was our school like and who was the principal? And our home: How was it furnished and what did our parents do? Can you believe it, our parents were the great grand-parents of our twenty-year-old grandchildren?

Descriptions, descriptions, descriptions—we can't have too many of them. Remember, the young man or woman who comes to visit us now may never have seen a streetcar, ridden in a horse cab or owned a windup gramophone.

Next we go on to the happenings: our love affairs, sports achievements (and heroes), school activities, plays we saw, even the books we read and the songs we sang. Does anyone sit around a campfire anymore, toasting marshmallows on the end of a pointed stick? Often the most unremarkable occasion will make the most engrossing reading. Room for another aside? When I started writing about the past, I discovered to my surprise that my most memorable occasions in the period just after World War I were my Saturday afternoons at the movies.

Young people today, and I don't mean just those in their teens or twenties but many in their thirties and forties, are totally unaware of the audience excitement generated by a silent black-and-white movie in which the firing of a gun was indicated by a wisp of muzzle smoke, and important conversations appeared in on-screen captions. No soap opera compares for thrills to the *Perils of Pauline*, which Saturday after Saturday found Pearl White, the beauteous heroine, tied to the rails as the steaming locomotive approached, or hurtling over the cliffs in a Model A Ford, leaving all of us, young and old, in a state of exhaustion not to be remedied until the next week's installment when we watched her miraculous escape.

Better by far than any rock band or singer was the genius at the piano who played as the cowboys and the U.S. cavalry rode on screen and chased the Indians off, or who thumped the bass when the villain crept in and swept the high keys as the lady in peril was caught in the arms of the handsome, straw-hatted hero. At the keyboard, week after week, unrecognized, certainly underpaid, was our Rachmaninoff who never, never missed a cue and gave us, in those far-off days, all the mystery and excitement of sound. Where would Theda Bara, Fatty Arbuckle, Mary Pickford, Charlie Chaplin, and the Keystone Cops have been without the piano player?

FROM THE CIRCUS TO CHAUTAUQUA

One of my first assignments as a cub reporter on a metropolitan daily was in another equally nostalgic entertainment field. I was to get up at 5:00 A.M., take a trolley to the fairgrounds and come back with a story about setting up a circus. Barnum and Bailey—or was it Ringling Brothers or Sels Floto?—were back in town.

The local populace was eager to read all about the Greatest Show on Earth, and I had been chosen oracle to describe it for them. I'd been to the circus before, of course. Every kid went to the circus in those days and, though we may have entered by crawling under the tent or serving as water boys to the animals to get a free ducat, we got as much of a thrill as did the cigar-smoking tycoons who occupied the best seats. I'd watched the parades along Main Street with the prancing horses, lions and tigers in their cages, and the steam calliope reminding everybody "There'll be a Hot Time in the Old Town Tonight."

I'd never imagined what went on when the Big Top was just a mass of rolled-up canvas, and the shouts of "Hey Rube!" would greet the arrival of local gawkers who were sometimes looking for trouble. Elephants that had been sitting on tubs and performing tricks in the ring, as I remembered them, were now construction workers, hauling wagons, building supplies, and circus furniture from railway cars to the tent site. Roustabouts were everywhere, putting pieces together like a jigsaw puzzle. As the smaller tents went up, sideshow freaks, aerial performers, and clowns waited patiently, midgets mingled with the bearded ladies, the India rubber man chatted to the snake charmer—all as if they were a group of local people waiting to go to the fair.

Most of us Seniors were circus fans when we were young. Some of us dreamed of running away, flying through the air with the greatest of ease, or riding with the cowboys in the rodeo ring. The ambitions may never have been realized, but the memories are still there. All we need do is translate them into words that will spell out the sounds, the smell, and the excitement of circus days.

For many, expecially in small towns on the prairies, there was the thrill of Chautauqua, that travelling cultural experience that brought us William Jennings Bryan and William Shakespeare's *Hamlet*, Stoddard and his famous travel lectures, and well-clothed singers and dancing girls. Many people in America in the twenties and thirties had never been inside a theater or a music hall; their only brush with education had been in small one-room schoolhouses. Chautauqua brought them a new world of which they had only dreamed.

Those who are still in their mid-fifties arrived in this world too late to enjoy this uniquely American institution. Some of them got a quick peek in 1984 when "Chautauqua Girl—a Love Story" appeared on public television. I'm sure some of us could do even better if we put our pens and typewriters to work and hauled out our cherished memories of evenings in the Chautauqua tent.

The trick is to make the memories work, not just let them idle around and amuse us for a time. And the more we work at it, the stronger our memories will become. Again, we put down all we can remember, higgledy-piggledy, unorganized, and without any attempt at continuity. Then we gradually bring it into shape, start getting it into story form, start thinking of a beginning and an end but always, *always*, remembering what it felt like. There are editors everywhere who'd welcome a good article on "The Day the Circus Came to Town" or "Chautauqua Times in Little Midtown" if it's written with feeling.

(You may not believe this, but after writing that last line, I shut off the electric typewriter, took a coffee break, and watched a television show. There on the screen was a handsome white-haired woman, certainly over sixty, being interviewed about her first book, *Chautauqua Comes to Canada.*)

We write down our memories, stare at them, organize them to sentences, paragraphs, and pages. We search for a theme—a plot if it's fiction—and gradually begin to come up with sentences, paragraphs, and pages that will let others look at the circus or Chautauqua the way we did.

Tales of the pioneers are another favorite editorial subject; even the radio stations like them. As the French say, *malheureusement*, we're old, but not quite old enough to rate as true pioneers. What the editors and radio producers want is tales of rough back-breaking hardship, and about the biggest hardship we ever had was finding our way at night to the outdoor privy when we went to the summer cottage. Believe it or not, we were the first of the "soft" generations.

If we put our memories to work even harder than usual, however, it's not impossible to come up with some hair-raising pioneer tales to tell. Secondhand ones, it's true, but genuine pioneer stuff all the same. We heard them first at grandpappy's or grand-mammy's knee. They were the old homesteaders, the men and women who felled the trees, tilled the soil, trudged across a continent looking for Eldorado, or they were immigrants from Europe who came to America, couldn't speak English, struggled in the garment factories, the coal mines, and the steel mills, sent us to school and made us into the bright able-to-write people we are today.

Their stories were repeated over and over again. We tired of them, were ashamed of them sometimes. Now we know better. We know they were the stuff of which dream stories are made—not dreams of what is to come tomorrow but dreams of what happened yesterday.

It isn't lack of material that keeps us from writing nostalgia and capitalizing on one of the booming literary markets of today. We have all that is needed, except maybe the energy, the patience, or the skill to put it on paper. And those may all be cultivated if only we have the will.

What we are writing about is *our* past as we remember it. But *our* past is every younger person's past, too. Many of them are as anxious to share in it as we should be to write about it. We can also serve them in a practical way.

HOW-TOS—WHY NOT?

Memories or, more properly, experiences, are often particularly worthwhile to pass on to others. For experience, they say, is the best teacher—if not your experiences, someone else's. We should be adept at writing how-to books or articles: how to raise prize cattle, how to refinish furniture, repair gasoline engines, cook gourmet dinners, plead a case at law, or swindle trusting widows. If our pre-retirement experience has been along any of those lines, or in other fields, then we have the makings of a book of instruction, motivation, or even entertainment.

How-to books are popular and come out in a never-ending stream. The world apparently is always on the lookout for books or articles that will tell people in their own simple language how to do something they've always wanted to do but probably never will. Whatever we did in life, whether we were very important people or just ordinary Sallys and Joes slogging it out day by day, we probably learned how to do something somebody else would like to do—and could if we tell them about it.

We built or restored a summer cottage. That's a popular practice today. Fifty years ago, America was busy tearing down the old and building the new; now even big corporations are busy tearing down the new and building the old. How do they do it? By carefully preserving stone by stone the old structures, re-creating everything that was once behind them, then putting the stones back in place until you'd never know they went away, except that they're clean now instead of grimy. Once rat-infested waterfront warehouses are now $200,000 condominiums for the wealthy.

Our project was less pretentious, but we learned some lessons we could pass on. We not only learned how to use an adze but we actually learned what an adze is. We discovered how to handle old beams that were ripe for termites and found out which was better for a roof, tin or wood shingles. (The answer was tin.)

With all that valuable information we can get at it again. Assemble the memories. Remember the mistakes, the disasters, and the triumphs. We can recall the day we found there was a basement under the summer kitchen and found an ancient tea pot intact, lid and all. Our whoops of delight would have indicated we had uncovered some ancient Roman artifacts, and for a month we read all we could find about "digs." We put them all in order, these tidbits of our restoration days, and we mix them with some long-remembered humorous, romantic, or tragic happenings and presto! We've got a how-to on renovating an old house. In the right hands, the material we have rediscovered could be a full-length novel. Eric Hodgins did it with his novel (and subsequent movie) *Mr. Blandings Builds His Dream House.* Why not we?

We all have tales of love, tragedy, treachery, and adventure in our memory boxes: sometimes events with which we were personally involved, sometimes those that engaged our relatives or neighbors or that we read about in the newspaper. Properly mined, our memories are an almost inexhaustible lode for our after-fifty manuscripts. Think of it: If we've been around a half century or more, we've had 21,900 days—and just as many nights—to remember. One good memory for every 100 days shouldn't be too much for any of us, and that would give us at least 219 usable remember-whens.

Not a bad stockpile for a beginning writer.

SEVEN

Be a Journalist, a Columnist, an Op-ed Page Philosopher

It is perfectly true that the words of a journalist are ephemeral; they go into the nether world of old files and are forgotten. But does not the same fate befall a good many books? Look at the back stacks of any great library. What a marvelous metropolis of the immortals is there.

Goldwin Smith (1881)

A retiree who wants to be a writer doesn't have to be a novelist, a playwright, or a poet. One doesn't even need to compose eloquent essays or biting bits of satire to qualify as a literary person. Many of us who like to think we are of literary bent would find writing a book, either fiction or nonfiction, a labor too long, too complicated, and, in the end, too hazardous if we dreamed of it being saleable. Yet we may have something to say and the itch to say it in print.

The practical alternative is to become a part-time journalist—a free-lancer, in the parlance of the trade. There we can have the best of two worlds. We can communicate in writing and be paid for it, and we can avoid the agony of long, arduous hours of composition for which we may never be rewarded either in cash or by seeing our words on paper. For reasons which will become obvious, hundreds of Senior Citizens have found exciting part-time careers in many journalistic areas that seem to have been created especially for them.

We may tend to think of journalism in terms of the big metropolitan dailies with their big-name writers and syndicated columnists or of television network news shows with commentators and correspondents who have become household names. But in the United States and Canada, there are more than 17,000 daily and weekly newspapers and trade and technical journals, hundreds of popular magazines that publish both long and short articles on almost every subject under the sun, and countless radio and TV stations broadcasting local, regional, and national news around the clock. Serving this vast communications network is an army of free-lancers, many of them well over fifty. It is quite possible that the news item that impressed us the most last week was not a flash from the Near East or Soviet Russia, or an inside story from Washington or Ottawa, but an item about a newcomer to our community who wants to organize a Neighborhood Watch to help reduce the number of break-ins, an item that was written by a local free-lancer and appeared in the give-away weekly paper that is tossed on our doorstep.

All journalists are not war correspondents, investigative reporters, or gossip columnists, and in our later years, without previous experience, we would be making a mistake if we thought we were headed for any of those glamorous and highly paid fields. Even the fact that eons ago, we were on the high school or college paper or served as summer reporters on our local newspapers, will not be much help in getting into the journalistic big time. There are, however, many other opportunities. Working within the ubiquitous communications industry are many thousands of men and women who earn, if not a living, at least welcome pocket money by picking up what appear to be trivial scraps of information, interviewing people whose fame is both limited and fleeting, and describing scenes that are far from unforgettable.

They may never make the pages of a *Who's Who in Journalism*, or be tapped to receive a Pulitzer Prize, but they would have satisfied Thomas Jefferson who, when in Paris, wrote to a friend back home in Washington: "Of political correspondents I can find enough, but I can persuade nobody to believe the small facts which they see passing daily under their eyes are precious to me at this distance. Continue then to give me facts, little facts such as you think everyone imagines beneath notice."

And Peter McArthur, a Canadian author who made a living writing about simple things, explained his success in *To Be Taken with Salt*, published in 1903: "The less there is happening," he wrote, "the more a truly great writer finds to write about."

The lowliest free-lancers, much though they may be cherished by editors with a sense of what creates circulation, are sometimes referred to by journalistic snobs as "hacks" or "journeymen," but they perform a useful function. Without them, many small and even quite large publications and radio stations would cease to exist.

Charles Anderson Dana, publisher of the *New York Sun*, made his oft-quoted assessment of what is news in 1882 when he wrote in an editorial: "When a dog bites a man, that is not news, but when a man bites a dog, that is news." Note that Dana didn't say that when Germany declares war on China, that's news. He used an illustration that would be understandable to and accepted as valid by all Americans. The big news is what happens in our own backyards. We who become neighborhood correspondents will be carrying on the great tradition of newspapering.

A FOUNDATION OF FREE-LANCERS

Free-lancers provide the solid foundation virtually all newspapers, magazines, and trade publications depend upon. They, and the news and commentary departments of radio and television networks and local private stations must rely, finally, upon having some free-lancer or "stringer" upon whom they can call, or who will come forth on his own and help provide the international, national, statewide, or community coverage a publication must have.

"Fire today destroyed the state's oldest chicken house, built at Punkin Corner in 1750 by George Washington's cousin. No one was injured. Pete Punkin, the owner, says it will never be rebuilt."

A little four-line item like that could have appeared in a metropolitan daily because of its statewide interest. A longer story giving some of the history of the old house and possibly accompanied by a photograph would have interested weekly papers, not only in Punkin Corner but in other parts of the state.

A ninety-second (approximately one and a half pages double-spaced) report read on the air would give a radio station "live" coverage and bring a possible request for more. An alert free-lancer could garner checks from maybe half a dozen outlets without committing the unforgivable—selling the same story to competing journals or stations.

The secret is in being vigilant, observant, and prepared with good information sources and lists of potential newspaper and radio-TV markets. It is in this local community area that the retired, newly-fledged journalist has the best chance to succeed. And it is a very good best chance, indeed, because it offers us a territory to cover in which we, better than the editor, publisher, or broadcaster, know what's new and have access to it.

For some of us, our pre-retirement experience and acquired knowledge may make it possible to enter a more rarefied journalistic realm. As retired political scientists or politicians, diplomats or professors, we might even be *asked* by an editor or publisher to write a weekly commentary on current political affairs. Or a radio or TV station might consider us good commentator material. Our by-line carries weight because of our reputation, and our opinions, whether controversial or not, are likely to attract readers and viewers who want to be informed rather than entertained. Our pay, while it is hardly likely to be munificent, will be as much or more than we would receive if we published a book of memoirs.

OPPORTUNITIES ON THE OP-ED PAGE

In this area lies our opportunity to become Op-Ed page philosophers, a highly desirable occupation for those of serious bent who believe that written and spoken words are too important to be left to the sensationalists or the frivolous. Much of the news and commentary published in our newspapers and aired by our radio and television stations is inevitably written, printed, or broadcast—and read or listened to—with desperate haste. To be first with the news is the cardinal objective; to listen to the news while driving to work or during coffee breaks at home, in the office, or on the factory floor, has become a national addiction. Editorial writers and radio and TV commentators try to make up for this fast-news obsession with their enlightened comments. But they, too, write under considerable pressure. Today's editorial deals with today's news; today's broadcast commentary covers this hour's happening

There is room for a slower, more thoughtful, and calmer approach. This has led many papers to introduce what they call Op-Ed (opposite editorial page) opinion sections, and the broadcast media to provide daily or weekly forums for independent discussion of a great variety of subjects. Contributors to these are university professors, architects, doctors, retired politicians, and other notables who can be persuaded to express their views literately, as well as no-name essayists who submit material, whether on tape or in writing, fit to be printed or aired.

That's where we come in. How do we go about securing that rather glorified part-time employment as authors of regular or occasional analysis or philosophical Op-Ed pieces, or as guest commentators on radio or television? First, we begin by having something to say. Even then, unless we're already well known locally, nationally, or internationally, we're not going to be sought out by the *New York Times* or the NBC network. They have the pick of the crop: They'll make the approach to the man or woman they want, the "recognized authority." If we were that sort, we wouldn't be reading this book; we'd be sitting back mulling over offers, with hordes of rewrite experts waiting in the wings to correct any grammatical slips or spelling errors we might commit.

But the *Times* is not the newspaper world; and NBC is not the sum total of the electronic universe. Wherever we live—even if it's in metropolitan New York—there are smaller, less well-known but nevertheless popular newspaper and radio and TV stations willing to settle for the not-so-famous, if these people have something to say and can say it well. E. B. White, for instance, became a national figure through his editorials in the Kansas City *Star*, and William Buckley is better known to public television viewers than to those who watch the big commercial networks. Both became "personalities" *because* of their writing and broadcasting and were not chosen for any preexisting fame.

If we aspire to become Op-Ed philosophers or electronic media pundits, we should study very carefully over an extended period of time the editorials *and* the contributed comments in the newspaper, and listen regularly to the commentators on our selected TV and radio stations. We may then either make ourselves known by writing and mailing thoughtful, carefully prepared *short* letters to the editor, or writing two or three full-length articles designed specifically for the Op-Ed page and submitting them for publication. For radio or TV stations, where voice is as important as writing, a short spoken commentary on a home recorder cassette, accompanied by a letter, could be submitted to the news director.

If, although not famous, we are reasonably well known in our own communities, we might try making an appointment with the appropriate editor to deliver our copy or cassette and discuss our submission in person. Before calling on any editors, though, we should have all pertinent information with us: details about our careers, our expertise, our reputations, publication background of any sort, and references. We've got forty or fifty years of experience to offer; let's make sure it's wrapped up in a saleable package.

MASTERING THE BASICS
Our name and reputation may help us sell, but our ability to write or communicate will determine how long we last. Our use of language must equal or at least come close to our fund of knowledge. Not all politicians or diplomats or retired corporation executives possess that ability. For too many years, their opinions have been expressed in speeches and articles written by speech writers and "ghosts." A fledgling editor may be a little surprised or shocked when he receives the first journalistic effort from a retired statesman whose public statements and pronouncements he has always admired for their lucidity and color, only to discover that the man simply cannot write a sentence in simple English.

Fortunately, most veteran editors are not easily shocked.

For those of us whose writing skills are lacking, there is an available remedy. As discussed in the last chapter, there are literally hundreds of classes and schools of journalism throughout the land, where even at our relatively advanced age it is possible to learn the rudiments of writing for the English-language press. What applies to those of us who dare seek entry to Op-Ed pages or to contribute learned and informed columns on our particular specialty applies also, in large measure, to anyone who wants to make a beginning in journalism after fifty.

There are no simple rules for newswriting, any more than there are simple rules for writing novels or poetry. But there are standards, and the better we learn to conform to those standards, the more acceptable our correspondents' reports will be. Within limits, every individual has a right to an editorial style of his or her own. Those limits are defined by the standards that are accepted in most editorial offices and are taught in good journalism schools.

Even the best professional journalists make mistakes, misuse words and phrases, commit grammatical errors and, worst offense of all, confuse their readers. So many, in fact, that for years, Theodore M. Bernstein, assistant managing editor of the *New York Times*, prepared regular bulletins on better English for the news staff. Called "Winners and Sinners," they were filled with illustrations of bad reporting by some of the world's highest paid journalists, all of them culled from regular editions of the *Times*. A selection of these slips that got by in the night was published in 1958 in a book called *Watch Your Language*, described as "a lively, informal guide to better writing, emanating from the News Room of the *New York Times*." Lively and informal it was, and it must surely have come as a surprise to aspiring journalists who read it as well as to the talented reporters and editors who unwittingly contributed to it.

Bernstein's career as a journalist's "language doctor" began when he was managing editor of a college newspaper. Jacques Barzun, a fellow student of Bernstein, wrote the introduction to *Watch Your Language*. It was "one of Mr. Bernstein's pleasant and exalted duties," Barzun wrote, "to mark up every day the issue just published and, by excoriating faults of style, form and proofreading, to award demerits whose uneven accumulation on various heads would in time eliminate the surplus of candidates for positions on the news board."

That is the practice Bernstein carried with him to the *Times* and which he was able to revive when he became assistant managing editor of that great newspaper. Again, in the words of Mr. Barzun, he performed a function "which is now neglected by every educated person in his role as parent, teacher or employer, quite as if the older practice of marking up texts and marking down slovenly writing had no purpose but to annoy. The truth is that unless some effort is made to arrest the black rot that we try to disguise by calling it 'the problem of communication,' it will presently bring us to the last stage of mutual incomprehension— that in which we think we understand one another when we do not even understand ourselves."

Since that's not a situation to which we would like to contribute, let's pay attention to some of Bernstein's cardinal rules that apply to all reporters, staffers *or* free-lancers. These are the things that Bernstein thinks are important:

1. Know what you're writing about.
2. Make what you are writing about easily understood by readers. Don't use terms and descriptions with which most people are unfamiliar.
3. Keep the lead or opening paragraph brief and lucid. Remember that maybe half your readers will go no farther than that first paragraph and that all they will know about what you are reporting will be in those first few lines.
4. Keep lead sentences short, but make each one say something that is vital to your story.
5. Do not editorialize. The public has a right to know what happened, not what you think about it. (This, of course, does not apply to those of us who are about to become pundits; our opinions may be just what the editor ordered.)
6. Avoid over-characterization. Good words to shun are "pretty," "attractive," and "beautiful."
7. Be careful about paraphrasing.
8. Explain, explain. Take it for granted your reader doesn't have any prior knowledge of what you are writing about.
9. Be concrete. Avoid the abstract.
10. Spell people's names right.

Short sentences are better, Bernstein believes, as are short, easily understood words. One-idea sentences are in most cases preferable to those that try to cover the whole waterfront. As an illustration, he quotes from a report appearing in the *Times*: "Dr. Samuel H. Sheppard, young, good-looking, prosperous osteopath whose hobbies are water-skiing and sports cars, is accused of beating his wife, Marilyn, to death in her bed in their surburban $31,000 home on the shore of Lake Erie early in the morning of July 4." As one reader remarked, "Shouldn't the sentence have told what kind of oil burner was in the cellar?" I'd go further and say that the reporter should also have dragged in the Declaration of Independence since the deed was performed on the Fourth of July.

There are a hundred or more journalistic crimes perpetrated by *Times* reporters and quoted in Bernstein's book, covering everything from what he describes as "hearts and flowers writing" ("The spiritual beauty of Christmas became an eternal reality today for Mike Korcheck, 24-year-old shortstop with the Brooklyn Dodgers' farm team at Fort Worth, Texas." Translate: Mike Korcheck died.) to gobbledygook ("improved financial support and less onerous work loads. . ." Translate: higher pay and less work.)

THE NEWSROOM IN THE COMPUTER AGE

Newspapering is a very different profession today than it was when we were young and, perhaps, served an apprenticeship on a local or a college paper before beginning our full-time careers. Today's reporters often tell me they are heartily sick of the Big Businessman or Businesswoman or the hail-fellow-well-met politician who starts an interview by saying: "I used to be a newspaper reporter and worked on the *Daily Blah* back in the thirties." It's like somebody telling a worker in a computerized, robot-operated car factory that he once worked in a carriage plant, making slots for buggy whips. Newspaper staffs today work in clean, modern, sometimes beautiful newsrooms, surrounded by computers and word processors like almost any other business office. The old "scoop" mentality that made newspapering and newspaper stories and films so exciting in the days of Walter Winchell and Ben Hecht has almost completely disappeared.

The hustling young newsboy who tipped off the police reporter to an imminent bank heist is no longer the hero of the newsroom. Journalistic expertise is not the exclusive property of ambulance chasers and sob sisters. Other qualities and skills are more in demand. Financial page reporters are frequently M.B.A's (Masters of Business Administration) who know all about cash flow, disemployment of surplus workers, stockholders' indemnities, and take-over tactics. Writers for the section headed "Living" (as opposed to "Dying," I suppose) may be trained sociologists, home economists, or professional decorators, while doctors or others with medical backgrounds write medical news; science reports are frequently prepared by men and women with scientific backgrounds who prefer the newsroom to the laboratory.

Those of us who have specialized in any of those professions may quite easily find full- or part-time employment either on local newspapers or with radio or TV stations. As we become known as writers, we may also receive assignments from professional journals. This employment could continue as long as we're able to express our ideas and relate our experiences in readable prose. We must also understand, however, that we cannot write for a technical journal as we would for a newspaper, magazine, radio, or television editor. We must be able to translate technical information into layperson's language and write with the assumption that the people who read what we write will have, at best, the equivalent of an eighth-grade education in our subject.

That's enough about us "brain trusters," with fascinating experiences and amazing insight and foresight to support our weekly contributions. But there's also a field for us who have the urge to write, but no great tidings to impart. How do *we* make out, we who have no great reputations to take us past closed editorial doors and into the Op-Ed page and who must use whatever writing and leg power we possess to report on other people's doings? (Without giving even a hint of how we feel about it all.) Is there room for us?

Ronald J. Cooke, author of *Money-Making Ideas for Retirees*, thinks there is. He devotes an entire chapter in his down-to-earth little guide to opportunities for Seniors in photography and journalism and begins by citing himself as one of the best examples. Since he retired some ten years ago, short articles he has written, often accompanied by his own photographs, have appeared in more than 100 publications in the United States and Canada. He doesn't turn up his nose at the small country weekly or the big city community throwaway. They all use good old U.S. (or Canadian) currency, he says, and they're all in the market for the same kind of reports. Scarcely a week goes by that he doesn't get checks for anywhere from fifty to three hundred dollars, payment for some small items he picked up as he went about his daily rounds.

ONE FIRE—FIFTEEN STORIES

Cooke finds stories wherever he happens to be. He hears about a shopping plaza that burned down. Fifteen stores were destroyed. To most of us, that would be just another fire and, perhaps, we'd feel sorry for the merchants. To Cooke, it's fifteen stories for fifteen different trade papers—interviews with owners or managers on how much they lost and what they planned to do—and maybe fifteen more stories six months later if they re-open in new and in many cases quite different premises.

There may even be a newspaper feature among the lot. The owner of the jewelry store, for instance, could have been a refugee from Poland who brought with him a collection of family jewels that had been smuggled out of Russia. That collection gave him his start in a new country; his store was a success. Now it was gone, and he had neither the will nor the energy to start all over again.

An old lady who owns a travel agency gives Cooke two more stories, one for the local daily and a spin-off for a travel magazine. He might also have been able to sell a piece to one of the women's magazines, which are always looking for women's success stories.

Cooke is always working, and enjoys what he does. It keeps him outside, meeting people and learning about interesting events. The barber who cuts his hair is a potential story subject, so he opens up the conversation instead of waiting for the barber to start talking, as most of us do. At lunch in a restaurant, he spots a strange coffee-making machine and talks to the owner about it. Boom—another trade paper story.

One of the great prides of Cooke's life is his record of selling the same story to as many as a dozen different publications—never competing ones, of course. A report about a local shoe repairman, for instance, might be a good personality piece for a local daily; it's also just right for a national shoe trade journal. If the shoeman uses some special machinery, there's a story for a machinery magazine, and if he did some unusual advertising, a marketing editor could also be interested. Finally, there's the possibility a business magazine would be a market prospect and a medical journal could use an angle on care of the feet.

In writing the same story for different publications or for the electronic media, all basic facts remain the same. There was a fire; a shopping plaza burned. That becomes the lead for a story to the local daily, followed by a listing of the various establishments that were destroyed, an estimate of total damage, and so forth. Then the several different elements are separated, each element being emphasized in a new report for a special publication. For the shoe journal, we'd write: "Hot Shot Shoe store's local outlet in the Boomtown Shopping Plaza was completely destroyed when the center burned down January 2. One of the best-known retail shoe outlets in the area, it featured a large repair department and was the exclusive distributor of Top Fit shoes, manufactured by Oliver Shoe Company of St. Louis, Mo." We'd continue with any other interesting details about the gutted shoe outlet that would appeal to the shoe journal's readers who are associated with the shoe trade and include Hot Shot suppliers and competitors.

For the advertising magazine, we'd write the story like this: "A retail shoe store that built up a statewide business through radio advertising went out of business last month when it was destroyed in the Boomtown Shopping Plaza fire. Tony Moreno, the proprietor, did his own commercials, frequently pausing in the midst of a plug for his merchandise to sing a line from an Italian opera. 'He was one of the best entertainers we had on the air,' station manager Jim Blatz told *Ad News and Views*, 'and we're thinking of hiring him to put on an act until he can get his store opened in a new location.' " Facts about the fire can follow.

Ronald Cooke reminds me of a German cartoonist I knew who used to live on Long Island and is now back in a mountain chalet just outside Munich. While Cooke sees everything and everybody as a potential news story, Gerhard Brinkman saw everyone and everything as a possible cartoon. One evening, my wife and I and the Brinkmans went to a ballet at Lincoln Center. It was an excellent performance by a world-class company and we were greatly impressed. But it was not until we went to a restaurant for an after-theater snack that we had a look at the ballet through Brinkman's eyes. He produced his sketchbook and showed us five or six roughly-drawn cartoons featuring the ballerina, the corps de ballet and the principal male dancer. Two of them he sold to an American magazine and one to a humor publication in Germany.

Brinkman enjoyed the ballet (he was also a concert pianist before the war). But, like everything and everybody else, ballet and ballet dancers were, first of all, potential cartoon characters. Those of us who choose to become free-lance journalists must learn to view the world around us, and its occupants, as one- and two-line headings and sticks of type.

It all sounds so easy. But like so many other things in the writing business, being a successful free-lancer requires some special writing skill, some knowledge and understanding of what we are writing about and a knowledge, too, of the market we serve—the newspapers and magazines for whom we are writing and the people who read them. In other words, it's not just a bit of fun, it's a unique craft with its own rules and regulations. It calls for a strong sense of observation and a willingness to go around with our eyes wide open. It's also a help if we like using the telephone and keep a long and ever-growing list of "contacts" whom we feel safe in calling at any hour of the day.

BIG FISH IN LITTLE PONDS

"But I live in a big city," you say, "and the local newspapers and radio and television stations have big staffs and cover all the news. They don't need any help from me."

Go to the bottom of the class! How many staff writers do you think work for the *Willowdale Weekly Express*, that runs "all the community news that we can find to print"? Well, there's Elsie Broadbent, who's the editor—and I guess she's the owner, too. Then there's Jim Broadbent, her son; he goes to high school but sits in as news editor Wednesday nights when the paper's going to press. There's Effie Brown: retired, used to be a telephone operator, got too old; she's on a pension. She bought a small camera and she's the paper's photo-journalist. Most of the copy, Effie writes.

So they don't need any help?

There are hundreds and hundreds of small community weeklies, and not all of them are in small towns or villages. Some of them serve residential communities in big cities, or suburbs that have their own shopping plazas and retail streets, with advertisers who are happy to have a local paper in which they may advertise their merchandise. And wherever there's anyone who wants to advertise, you'll find someone publishing something for them to advertise in.

Most of us may sometimes laugh at the eight-pager that is stuck in our letter box once a week even though we may never pay for it. But we look at it just the same, and now and then we come across a piece of local news that the big papers never published. So we keep looking. It's those little pieces that make the give-away paper, and other community weeklies, successful, because in the long run, they've got to have readership as well as just circulation. The local advertiser knows if they're read or not. If he doesn't, he won't be long in business.

Alongside the community newspapers are the community radio stations, and the community program directors on the larger stations who find that concentrated local news periods draw listeners.

We all know about the married couple who divided their responsibilities. The woman looked after the minor details, like cooking the meals, making the beds, seeing that the rent was paid, hiring the gardener, and hearing the kid's school lessons. Papa attended to the important affairs, like what Russia was doing in Afghanistan, if Britain would go off the gold standard, and what men were discovering on the moon.

Well, our local paper's like the woman of the house. It's interested in what our next-door neighbors are doing up on the roof with a small pile driver and a half mile of wire cable; it's interested, too, if some local resident has produced the biggest carrot in state history. What we or our neighbors do interests the editor and readers of the *Community Bugle.* The same goes for radio station WHOO that's on the hunt for local ratings.

That's where we come in. The editor's a pretty nice person, but can't know everybody in town. And the paper's budget is too small to allow for a dozen reporters to scour the streets and check everybody's backyard. Knowledgeable free-lancers with time on their hands are the answer—and that's us. If we're going to become one of the editor's trusted "stringers," we must let him, or her, know we're available, that we're willing to work, and that we know our way around the area.

We may have to do a little experimental reporting on our own, then call the editor with stories we think might be of interest. Like the big-shot authority looking for a spot for his or her behind-the-scenes articles, we need a few samples. The place to get started on these, of course, is in a journalism class or with a correspondence-course instructor. Then, with confidence, we can march into the newsroom and display our wares.

If we take in our little items, properly written, clean-typed and ready for the printer, chances are good we'll at least get a call. That "ready for the printer" remark is more important than it sounds. Once upon a time, correspondents handed in their stories hand-written on old scraps of paper, just making sure they had names spelled right. The rest was up to the weary editor. Today, many small dailies and weeklies are printed "offset," the copy typed in newspaper-width columns, pasted into place on the news page, photographed, and the plates sent to the press room to be printed. If we're really skilled and can sit down and write to exact specifications, or use a word processor that can justify type, we're the answer to a community editor's prayer.

That takes care of the community paper which is only one of the media that can and do make use of a first-time journalist's services. Let's visit the local library and go through the newspaper and magazine directories in the reference section. If we live in a small or big-city suburb, we should take down the names of nearby metropolitan newspapers, radio and TV stations. They may have local correspondents already. If we seem to have something special to offer, such as, we're Senior Citizens and not likely to quit to take the first full-time job that comes along, or we're Senior Citizens and have lived in this town for fifty years (used to be mayor, or clerk in the liquor store, and know everybody by first name) we may be taken on as backup to the existing correspondent, and that's a foot in the door. And if we sit down and talk things over seriously with newspaper editors or radio-TV producers, we'll find that there are many holes unfilled. No newspaper that I know of has ever had a 100 percent complement of correspondents. There's always room for one or two more.

We go back home and think, what can we do for that nice editor who said he'd call me if he needs me? Well, we can help him need us. If we check the newspaper, or listen to the radio station, we'll see that every now and then there's a story from a small-town council meeting, or a small-town crime report, items about odd personalities, strange by-laws—human interest stories of all sorts. Those stories didn't get there by accident. They were either clipped from a local, noncompetitive weekly or sent in by a correspondent who was able to distinguish between news of purely local interest and that which might appeal to big city readers. After all, most big city people came from small towns and they like to read—and perhaps laugh—about the country yokels they left behind. If it amuses them, that's fine, as long as there's a check for us at the end of the line. So if we go to a meeting, or talk to an interesting citizen, and the regular correspondent isn't there, we get our story in fast. Before long, they'll be calling us.

Using one's hobby or special interest is another way to gain entry to local newspapers and possibly even a network of publications including the craft or hobby magazines. Just suppose we're one of the millions of people who collect rare postage stamps and paste them in albums. Since we've been around a long time, there are probably things we know about stamps and collecting that are not known to most of our fellow collectors.

SPECIAL INTEREST REPORTING

In our community, there are a few hundred of us. They make just as valuable readers as people who play golf or go to football games, yet nobody on the newspaper, at least, seems to bother about them. Until we arrive, that is . We suggest that we write a weekly stamp column—not one of those big-name syndicated columns they can get for almost nothing, but a column aimed at the specific interests of collectors in our area and featuring local names and local collections. We won't charge much, either, because we know if the column catches on, we can peddle it to half a dozen or more regional papers and might even talk the hometown editor into running off proofs for us each week so that our only extra cost will be postage.

If you think that nothing very spectacular or rewarding is likely to result from all this, take heart and be prepared to study the story of Erma Bombeck, America's ace woman humorist who made it to the front cover of *Time* in 1984. In the early sixties when, she says, she was "too old for a paper route, too young for Social Security and too tired for an affair," housewife and mother Bombeck began writing a column for the Kettering-Oakwood *Times*, a suburban weekly of the kind we've been talking about. For each column, written at a desk made of a piece of plywood supported by cinderblocks set up in her bedroom, she received three dollars. In 1965, the Dayton *Journal Herald*, attracted by the K-O *Times* columns, asked her to write a twice-a-week column. Then the *Newsday* syndicate signed her up and a year later, she was appearing in thirty-six newspapers. Not only was she in the money, she was urged by publishers to write a book; that was the beginning of still another career, as a published author. And it all began with a 500-word column in a small town weekly, a column about her "hobby," which happened to be raising a family and cooking meals.

What applies to hobby writing applies equally to other activities in which we may be interested. We may be football nuts; perhaps we coached the high school team in its glory days when it went all the way to the state championship. We could either cover individual games, or write a football commentary; publishing stories under our by-line as "former head coach, Little Barnstable High School, 1951 champions," the paper might have a ready-made audience. There's an added advantage to the paper in having us as its "football correspondent." Right now, it probably depends on local clubs sending in their after-game reports. Not a very satisfactory system. If a club gets walloped one Saturday afternoon, the captain or the club manager isn't going to rush downtown to make sure the local paper gets the story first. And the winner of a regional school championship may be too whipped up with enthusiasm and pride to worry about meeting the *Weekly Bugle's* deadline.

If the *Bugle* had someone like us, someone who understands the game, knows how to report it and regards reporting it as a job, has a respect for deadlines and covers the bad with the good, it would probably fork out a few bucks a week for the privilege. We might even get a press pass to the playoffs.

We're good for reporting sports, good for covering women's club activities (didn't we used to be head of the Women's Association for Political Reform?), acquainted with homemaking, craft organizations, art groups, church and social organizations. We've been around a long time and have the contacts. No one has to tell us where to go to find the information we need.

Writing for the community press requires the same high standards as those of the big-city dailies. We can't be long-winded; space is limited. Yet we can sometimes write longer articles than would be acceptable in a big paper crowded with so-called *impor-*

tant news (like who's ahead in Afghanistan). We must learn to keep our biases and our prejudices to ourselves and to report fairly, yet make use of our knowledge to write more than just bland reports.

BREAKING INTO BROADCASTING

What works with community newspapers will also work with community radio and television stations. The same editorial requirements exist, with the added necessity for speed when working for the broadcast media. Community program directors want local news, local names, and local controversies because that's the only thing they can use to draw listeners or viewers away from the networks. Nobody's going to tune in a third-rate movie on television station PING if NBC, CBS, or ABC has a first run blockbuster being premiered. But people will switch, even in prime time, if they know a local station is going to broadcast the results of a dog show in which they and most of the neighbors have canine entries.

If Mrs. Hometown's daughter—the one who sings—wins a scholarship and is offered a part in a Minneapolis musical, that's hot news in our town and the local radio or TV news department may be happy to get it first. The station that has a strong community news department is going to get local listeners and viewers. If we help them get that news, we can be stringers for them and they'll be glad to have us.

Special training for radio or TV newswriting is important. We can get it at some journalism schools, or we can read any one of a number of how-to books (listed in the Bibliography) that will give us the essentials. Basically, we must learn to write as we talk, because we'll be writing for talkers. We must condense, because twenty seconds on the air is like a half column in a newspaper. We must present facts clearly and in logical order because, unlike the newspaper reader, the *average* radio or TV listener cannot turn back and check what they have just read. I say *average* because the introduction of video recorders makes it possible to do just that—put an item away and go back and hear it or look at it later.

Seniors attracted by the electronic media are by no means restricted to small-time local outlets, though those admittedly are the best prospects for beginners. In both the United States and Canada there are national network programs mindful of the rural and small-town backgrounds of many of even their sophisticated and urban listeners. National Public Radio's "All Things Considered," a daily news program, occasionally features short interviews with and reports from "ordinary Americans" across the country, commenting on everything from the strangeness of becoming a first-time father, to the change of the seasons in Michigan, to gathering mushrooms or making bark tea without wiping out your family in the process. These items, some live and some on tape, can reflect any aspect of altering lifestyles, or preservation of old ones, all based on volunteered comments by people across the country. Some especially interesting commentators have "appeared" several times—brought back, one assumes, by popular demand. In Canada, listeners to "Fresh Air," a Sunday morning radio feature on CBC, hear a half-hour program called "Voice of the Pioneers," which consists of interviews with octogenarians and some even older who recall the days that used to be.

How do radio and TV programmers find the old-timers to do the talking? Sometimes, they pick names out of the weekly or small-town daily press. Sometimes an alert old-timer writes or telephones them offering to go on the air; he sends along a sample cassette so the programmers can tell both if the Senior has a good "radio voice" and if the comments are likely to interest the audience.

The late-night national TV news program in Canada ends with a ninety-second commentary called "The Last Word." In January, 1985, as I sat worrying about my income falling due to a drop in interest rates, I thought of the number of Senior Citizens with a similar problem. I wrote a page and a half diatribe against the perpetrators of this crime against thrifty retired persons who had saved their money so they could live comfortably in their old age. I sent it to the program director for "The Last Word." Two days later I received a telephone summons to go to the local CBC office and put my message on video tape. The next night I watched myself (a humbling experience) haranguing fellow viewers. At month's end, a check for $185 arrived; not bad for half an hour's work!

Movie, play, and book reviewers are regular fare on local and national radio and TV, and not all stations are willing or able to pay for professional, full-time reviewers. They are receptive to submissions from qualified amateurs. There are openings, as well, for part-time sports, bridge, gardening, and hobby commentators. The way to get there is to become a radio/TV addict for a month or longer. Study the air waves as you would study the newspaper or magazines you'd like to write for. Read radio/TV listings; scrutinize magazines like *TV Guide*; listen and watch at all hours of the day. A program that might be ideal for us could come on at 5:00 A.M. or 1:00 P.M. Video recorders will help us build up a file of samples of our type of program; audio tape recordings we make of radio correspondents' voices will help us prepare our own cassettes.

Even cable channels might provide us with a start. Many cable channels supply facilities for local community affairs and cultural programming broadcast at no extra charge to all the cable subscribers. Look at the listings in the cable guide. Is there a program made by and featuring local people sharing their views and insights? Maybe the amateur producer of that program would be happy to hear from us. Or, if we're really ambitious, we could contact the cable company itself and find out what would be involved in becoming producers ourselves, developing our own show or series available to thousands of subscribers.

The electronic media are seemingly inexhaustible: radio and TV stations use up news and talk and fun and games twenty-four hours a day. Some of it might just as well be ours.

Our own communities present an interesting marketplace for our journalistic efforts, but as we become better at news reporting, we may raise our sights and see that, for many of the items we cover, there is a national, or even an international outlet. It's not impossible, for instance, to hook on as a space-rate correspondent for *Time* or *Newsweek*. We won't sell them a piece every week, or every month, but once or twice a year, a *Time*-type article may drop in our laps and we should be ready to take advantage of it. It could be a battle in the local Council chamber where the newly-elected woman mayor threw her predecessor out the window and was arrested by a new woman police chief for assault and battery. Six or eight lines, perhaps; maybe fifty dollars in our pocket! Or it could be an unusual medical discovery at the local hospital, an announcement about a new way of disposing of pig manure and saving our rivers from contamination, or an underwater marriage featuring a couple of snorkelers. Without people like us, these world-shaking events might never be recorded, and the readers of *Time* and *Newsweek* would be the poorer.

The extent and the success of our journalistic efforts are limited only by the bounds we put upon our own ingenuity and energy. If we try to correspond for publications beyond our community borders, or write for trade papers and general magazines that use quasi-journalistic features, story ideas will come from many sources. First are our own contacts, conversations with people we meet, information that comes to us by mail or telephone as neighbors learn that we are on the hunt. Next in importance are newspaper clippings; a paragraph in a newspaper about a district nurse who has organized a house-to-house health survey and discovered a near-epidemic of mumps could easily become a feature article, with photographs, in a medical magazine or a national woman's publication.

If we subscribe to area newspapers and do some local radio and TV monitoring, we may find usable, expandable items. We must look for the little fillers, the one-line headings on short bits that editors use to fill out columns. That's where I found the item about the grass-growing sheep; I just couldn't figure any publication that would like to buy a full-scale article and I wasn't about to go all the way to England to get photographs.

And speaking of photographs—the ultimate answer for the Senior correspondent may not just be journalism but photo-journalism. The two go together and by doing so, can triple or quadruple our income. We don't need to be professional photographers; using a good automatic focusing camera, we can get satisfactory prints. Payment for the photograph is a bonus, often exceeding the payment for the story itself.

STARTING YOUR OWN NEWSPAPER

Just as if we were about to write a short story or a novel, we should study the market for news-type articles and try to write what editors want. Most editors, during slack periods, are willing to discuss their general requirements, but we should realize that news and feature articles and photo opportunities abound all around us. There are editors as anxious to get news and features as we are to sell them.

Should all our efforts fail and every editor we contact turn us down, not because what we have to sell isn't saleable but because they cannot afford to pay, there is one interesting and adventurous course left open to us. We can decide to publish our own newspaper!

"Now," I hear you shouting, "that's enough. You've gone too far. Publish our own newspapers, indeed. Don't you know, it costs a fortune to publish a newspaper?"

I know. I know. But I also know of people who during the past few years have started their own newspapers, had a lot of fun running them, and have put money in the bank. It's not a project for Junior who has to put the kids through school, pay household bills, pay for a new car, and buy the groceries. It's ideal for a well-organized Senior Citizen—or better, Senior Citizen couple—who have a yen for journalism, a pension to live on, and the time, talent, and desire to become newspaper publishers.

No one knows how many suburban quarterlies, district newsletters, and apartment house "giveaways" are published in America. They're not listed in any directories, nor are they likely to win any prizes for journalistic enterprise, yet they are read, altogether, by thousands, perhaps millions, of North Americans, and supported by some hundreds, or thousands, of small merchants who can't afford to advertise in the big-time press. There could be one or ten thousand of them, some them published by retirees.

Who needs these little amateur efforts that come in assorted sizes? Some are printed on five by seven or eight by ten sheets; others are tabloid newspaper size. Typed and photocopied or mimeographed and printed, they are stuck willy-nilly under doors or into letter boxes of homeowners or tenants who never asked for them. Well, the advertisers do. The little corner store, the independent one-shop druggist, the hairdresser who works out of her home, the seamstress who makes wedding dresses, and the tailor who repairs men's pants and occasionally gets an order to design a suit or an overcoat—they all need some place where, at a cost they can afford, they can offer their services or merchandise.

Daily newspapers and even many weeklies are far out of reach for these small merchants, of whom, even in this chain-store age, there are thousands. The big retailers can advertise in dailies with full pages and whole sections for which they pay thousands of dollars. Small merchants have no way to fight back—unless someone comes along with a low-cost medium.

We, as budding journalists, can provide that medium in one of two ways. We can start by helping the merchant produce interesting and readable "fliers" that will tell his story and be read by recipients who throw most such literature in the rubbish heap. An article of local interest, followed by a short advertisement, would be read by many nearby residents and could be produced and distributed for much less than the cost of a newspaper ad. We would do the writing; it would be good practice and might even lead to our getting an appointment as a correspondent.

If our little feature article plus advertisement throwaway works for one merchant, why not for another? In a grocery store flier, we could write about food topics (nutrition, local recipes, reports of community dinners, barbecues, etc.). For the local florist, we'd produce a monthly flier about gardening, and so on.

Get three or four fliers going and we're on the way to having a community newspaper. Instead of printing and distributing them separately, why not cut costs and combine them in one publication? Presto, we're publishers.

Now, of course, we've taken over the whole production job and we're responsible for the printing as well as the writing. Let's ask each merchant to give us his production cost, including our small fee, and say that's the price he'll pay for an advertisement equal in space to the display ad he carried in the flier. Put the four or five merchants together and we've covered our printing and editorial costs. If we pick up some newcomers, that's gravy. We must, however, continue to keep our rates in line with our area merchants' limited ability to pay.

This may be great for a small town or village where there's no local paper, but what about us city dwellers? Everybody on our street gets the morning or evening daily, and sometimes both. They're not going to be bothered reading another giveaway.

That's up to us. We can make them read it if we give them the kind of news and information that interests them, and that they won't find in the *New York Times* or the *Chicago Tribune*. There are any number of "street papers" or "neighborhood news sheets" with editorial content restricted to what goes on next door. Where I once lived, an enterprising resident published *The Gables Court Reporter*. Circulation: 51 families living in the court; news content: articles about activities around the community swimming pool, home renovations, parties, Mr. Smith's new car, and Mary Edwards's appointment as assistant to the town engineer. Search the columns of the city's *Evening Star* and you'd never find a line about any of these "important" local happenings. Small merchants a mile and a half away in the shopping plaza were happy to have a chance to address residents in this small area—at a cost not much greater than the price of a pound of beef.

It's a bit like self-publishing a book—without the financial risk and with a real chance for a little profit. And if we're still anxious to see that short story in print, there's no reason why we can't try it out on our *Neighborhood-Blah* readers. One of them might even turn out to be a publisher's rep who'd find it interesting enough to invite us to pay him, or her, a visit.

We can start out as amateur journalists, looking for a place to settle, become part-time correspondents, and end up as publishers, TV producers, editors, feature writers, reporters, commentators—the works.

EIGHT

Try Writing With...

*You may share the labors of the great,
but you will not share the spoil.*

Aesop (550 B.C.) from *The Lion's
Share*, a fable that can sometimes
be proved demonstrably untrue.

It's one of the ironies of the writing profession that all who can write cannot necessarily sell, not even if they write very well.

In the business world, they say, it isn't *what* you know but *who* you know. In the writer's world, it's frequently not how you *write* but who you *are*.

And who says it was different three and four hundred years ago? I read somewhere that Shakespeare was always on the hunt for a noble patron, if only to be sure he wasn't hauled off to the pokey for offending some high and mighty personage on stage. And Jane Austen had her first novel published because Daddy knew the publisher. (She didn't even want to be seen in print but her old man was determined, and in those days parental wishes were backed up by authority.)

You and I may have all sorts of good stories clamoring to be told and may have studied and taken creative writing courses and read good books until literary aphorisms are running out our ears and still not be able to find anyone willing to publish what we write.

Editors may even like what we offer them and assure us we have all sorts of talent. They could be disappointed that they're going to have to let a promising writer like us get away. But there are those old bogeymen—the public and the bank. Men and women are less likely to buy books written by people they never heard of. Editors who have sent me rejection slips have given this as the main reason. "Your book's just fine," they write. "Enjoyed reading it and found it very interesting. But you're just not famous, or infamous, and we could find ourselves losing maybe $10,000 for the doubtful pleasure of publishing a fine book by a nonperson." A thousand times better they should publish a nonbook by man, woman, or child of ill fame!

So, how do we get famous so we can get to publish our *Lives and Loves* or the *Amazing Career of . . .* ? We don't. At least not overnight. We go looking for someone who *is* famous, or notorious, and then ride to success on his or her back. We write a book with a famous person. We just make sure that when it surfaces it carries not only the by-line of our newfound benefactor but ours, too, on the front cover in discernible type.

There are ghosts and *ghosts;* at the end of this chapter, we'll go deeper into the subject of "unsubstantial" ones. We no longer take our famous person's ideas or life story, put them or it into good readable English and then hang his or her name on it. We submit it to a publisher as a "written with. . . ." When our "ghosted" book appears, as it will if a publisher thinks our collaborator is famous enough, it will stand up on the shelf in shiny, impressive hard covers as:

Seven Thousand Gall Bladders
By the Eminent American Extractor
of Useless Appendages
DR. A.B.C. SURGEON
with
Who Else but Little Old Us

We're in the small type, sure enough. But we're up there for all the world to see, particularly that part of the world that is engaged in publishing things like *Books in Print* or entering library catalogue cards. If we're on the cover we get half the double-billing; inside on the title page, and we're lost to posterity like those "ghosts creeping between the lines" that Henrik Ibsen saw when his character picked up his newspaper in the first act of *Ghosts*.

BELIEVING IN GHOSTS

Most of us are familiar with ghost writers even if we don't know who they are. We sometimes suspect them of being present even when they're not, because we can't believe a movie star or a racing car driver can write well enough to get published when we can't. We're sure somebody wrote it for them. We know for sure that Winston Churchill wrote his own histories and memoirs, because he was a famous journalist long before he was a prime minister and nobody could copy his tremendous if overbearing command of English. But we're doubtful about those by old-soldier President Dwight Eisenhower or Harry Truman. Somehow, they didn't strike us as being all that literary. But their books appeared as "by" them, so maybe we're wrong.

Anyway, what we're interested in is writing a book well—one that may even be praised by the critics for its style as well as its content, because that's what we've been learning to do. Perhaps we might even get a gentle pat on the back, and the next time, or the next next time, we can go to a publisher with a book or books of our own, written by US, co-author of *Seven Thousand Gall Bladders* or whatever.

We won't be the first in this field, by any means. Millions of readers have read books by Leonard Felder, a "with-someone" writer who doesn't worry about having his own name alone up front, but is satisfied with doing a good job and making a good living. One of his books, *Learning to Love Forever*, with Adelaide Bey, was published by Macmillan. You may say "who's Adelaide Bey? She's not famous or well known, not to me, anyway." She may not be famous but she has a reputation in the field of psychotherapy, which makes her an authority on loving someone forever. Another book co-written by Felder, *Making Peace With Your Parents*, with Dr. Harold Bloomfield, a well-known psychologist, was picked up by Random House. "A famous name (belonging to someone else) gets you over the *must be famous* slip," Felder said in an article in *The Writer* in which he also referred to others in the same line: Kenneth Libo, co-author of *World of Our Fathers*, with Irving Howe, and Curt Gentry and Ken Hurwitz, whose suspense novels have been co-written with Vincent Bugliosi.

Still another "with-someone" writer, this time a bona fide retiree, is Henry Lebensold of Tamarac, Florida. Mr. Lebensold is a retired vocational guidance counselor. He guided himself into a post-retirement career as a writer and, encountering the same kind of obstacles we have witnessed above, he spent several years as a collaborator. One project, a book written with a physician/psychoanalyst, was about diet and mental health. And perhaps the most successful in this group of writers are Sammon S. Baker and Mickey Herskowitz who between them have co-operated with "big names" on books that have sold a total of more than 10,000,000 copies. Baker has more than twenty self-help books (including *The Scarsdale Diet*) with his lower case by-line, while Herskowitz has concentrated on personalities like Gene Autry and Howard Cosell.

Lebensold has added a new string to his bow and formed a "press center" to help all frustrated writers, particularly seniors. "If you are a professional writer cramped by commercial restrictions," he writes in a letter to *Seniority—the magazine for mature minds* (meaning us), "an aspiring writer unable to sell your output, a compulsive writer wasting your talents on letters to the editor, a correspondence freak, a barroom poet, a visionary with ideas begging to be heard, send your material to me after exhausting every effort to place it elsewhere. I will make a modest investment to give it exposure in an experimental publication slanted for people isolated in our superstar culture.

"Some may make it big, a few may shine in elitist groups, but literary competence is widespread and hidden where it can't be seen. Through a press center of this kind, persons of compatible interests, though living far apart, may also meet, exchange views and befriend one another." Interested? You can reach Mr. Lebensold at P.O. Box 25441, Tamarac, FL 33320 and find out what he has in mind.

Big movie stars and famous international characters choose their own ghost writers or have them thrust upon them by big successful publishers eager to get books with big names on them. They're not going to approach you or me for the same reason that publishers aren't fighting to get us on their spring or fall lists in the first place. To be a big-time ghost, you've got to be famous as a ghost; and you get to be that by doing something we haven't done, like having a best-selling book published.

Authors of best sellers could, if they wished, write a famous name biography, put their own names on it, drop it in at their publisher's office and have a good chance of having it published. We, on the other hand, can't expect the same reception. We must look for someone in a field with which we are at least partly familiar or in which we have more than just a casual interest. Not all "famous people" are that famous, as we noted when commenting on Leonard Felder's co-authored books. Some are just a little bit famous, yet what they have to say could be of interest to a great many people. If we examine the library and bookshop shelves we'll find dozens of titles like *Seventy Ways to Become a World Champion High Diver* by Elsie Slimmer, Olympic diving winner, or *Forty Years in the Pits* by Jimmy McKoo, king of the speedway mechanics. A lot of them should have "by-with" by-lines. Some do, but some are 100 percent ghosted; a very few are original.

While I was writing this a young, six-foot-six Englishman called to ask me what he should do about a book he had written on fox hunting in Britain and Ireland. "It's full of anecdotes—lots of funny stories," he said, "and information about hunting, too." He was quite right; he's an expert fox hunter but an amateur writer, and he couldn't find a publisher. His manuscript was just screaming for a co-writer.

The late Dr. Wilder Penfield, known throughout the world as a brain surgeon and founder of the Neurological Institute, always nursed a desire to be a novelist. On his retirement, he presented a publisher with a historical novel about a physician in ancient Greece. Because it was written by the famous neurologist and would have his name on the cover, the book would have a large ready-made audience, so it quickly found a publisher who should have known better. Reviewers, out of respect for the renowned scientist, treated the book gently; the reading public less so. It was not long before copies became available on the remainder counters in discount bookshops.

Dr. Penfield was a great surgeon. He had contributed much to medical knowledge. After his death, a boulevard in Montreal was named after him. His novel was based on a subject in which he had a personal interest. He simply couldn't write a good novel. The brain, whose actions he had studied, refused to perform for him the way he wanted. If he felt he had to create his romantic story, he might have done better to have worked with a professional ghost.

IN SEARCH OF THE CELEBRATED

Since famous people are unlikely to come to us to write their books for them, how do we go about finding a person who is well enough known to open editorial doors for us?

We can begin by looking around right at home. If we live in Oshkosh, Chicago, or beautiful downtown Burbank, it's certain we're not going to travel all the way to New York, or Montreal even, to find a second-class celebrity who's willing to have us as his or her Boswell. If there is someone we're really hepped on— like a ready-to-retire ballerina—and we're all-out balletomanes, a long trip might be justified, or at least a letter exposing our knowledge of and interest in dancing. Otherwise, we'd be better to check the famous people list at home.

Our old reliable sources—clipping services, newspapers, and magazines—are as reliable as any. Suppose we're fairly knowledgeable about dentistry—studied it for a year before quitting and joining a brokerage house in the Depression; or we have some knowledge of auto-dynamics, play tennis, have campaigned for day care centers. We watch for bright names to appear connected with any of these activities. Magazines like *People, Time, American Dental Journal*, and newspapers like *The Wall Street Journal* are fruitful sources. They have personality columns and are always quoting or running profiles on prominent people. And the hometown papers—daily and weekly, big city and community— parade the homegrown talent wherever it may be.

If we're knowledgeable in any of these fields, we must have some leads of our own, i.e., we know someone who is active in one of those areas. The search may not be easy, but it will be successful if we keep at it regularly.

Finally, one day we'll pick up a publication or clipping, or get a telephone call from a friend, and learn that the "darling of the tennis courts," Angela Twingling, is about to retire. That sweet little girl who was blowing them off the courts when she was fifteen (it seems like only yesterday) is about to become one of the tennis world's Senior Citizens at thirty-five! Tomorrow afternoon, she's playing in her last tournament, getting ready to serve her final ace.

She lives not too far away. We give her a call and make an appointment to see her. "Miss Twingling," we say, "thousands of American tennis fans have followed your sparkling career. They'd like to read your own story about your days on the tennis courts and nights in the ballroom on all those fascinating world travels. They'd like some tips, too, on how to become a 'darling of the tennis courts.' "

Miss Twingling probably thinks we're a publisher calling and says: "But I couldn't write a book; I didn't even pass my English exams in high school."

"No problem," we reply. "Maybe you couldn't write it—but we could. You tell us all about it and we'll put it into a book that someone will publish and people will buy. We can split the proceeds—say 60 percent to you, 40 percent to us, because you're the *important* part of the deal."

If Miss Twingling then responds as she should, we, or our lawyer, will draw up a contract. We'll give no guarantee of publication, unless we have a publisher's signature on the line, but will put the division of spoils on an if-and-when basis. If we don't guarantee publication, and haven't even had anything of our own published, she may very well ask what makes us think some editor is going to recommend purchase of her book just because our name's on it, too? Our answer is to produce our encouraging rejection slip (or a copy of this book) and say, here it is in black and white. To be published you've got to have a famous or infamous name, but you've also got to be able to write. The note from the publisher says we can write but, he's sorry, we're not famous. Our creative writing class teacher says, "You write very well," but nobody buys. Now, Miss Twingling, you've got the name. Together, we can win in straight sets. She's won over by our argument, and the story of her life is underway.

If Miss Twingling turns out to be Twirling or Scott-Smith or Beckendorf, and she's been a big wheel in auto mechanics or buttonhole-making, our approach may be the same, but we should first investigate the market to find out if there's any solid interest in a book or an article on any of these subjects even under the byline of a well-known practitioner.

Checking library catalogues to see what's listed under the subject we're working on is a good beginning. Next, look at market reports in *Writer's Digest, The Writer, Canadian Writer's Journal,* and *Writer's Market* to see what publishers have recently shown an interest in looking at as book subjects, whether it be sports figures, auto mechanics, or buttonhole designers. Select a few more obvious ones and send the publishers a query: "Would you be interested in looking at the story of her life by Angela Twingling?" A tennis player could be easy (even editors play tennis) but an auto mechanic?

Should one of these "class B" celebrities encourage us to proceed, the next step is to prepare, with their co-operation, an outline of the proposed book or article, a well-written synopsis and analysis of the specialized consumer market in which it might be sold. In short, would anybody but Miss Beckendorf's closest relatives be interested in reading it? And how many relatives does she have? If that prognostication looks good, off we go by mail to the publisher who told us what good writers we were but didn't think we were that famous.

This may end up as three or four queries; the first publisher may not be quite as enthusiastic as he sounded at first. But if our newly acquired collaborator really does have a reputation and has something interesting to say, even to a specialized audience, our chances of finding a willing publisher are better than our chances of collecting on a two dollar ticket to win on any nag in a six-horse race.

After going this far and realizing that the writing business isn't all writing but an occupation that requires one to be a market researcher, merchandiser, and sales person before a book is published (and a TV performer, lecturer, and retail store dummy after publication!) we may begin the writing part.

THE ART OF COLLABORATION

We should now sit down with our writing partner, preferably in her luxurious home and, between sips of gin and tonic, sherry, or afternoon tea or coffee, map out a program of interviews (on tape is best), go through scrapbooks, letters, and any other memorabilia she garnered during her career. We should then talk to her friends and former associates, get quotes from people who had dealings with her and who are also authorities in her field. Above all, we must worm our way into her personality, learn how she thinks and reacts and talks. For the next few weeks or months, every time we punch the capital *I*, it's not going to be *we* talking, it's going to be *she*. That won't always be easy, particularly when we have *I* saying something with which we personally violently disagree.

From the outset, we must establish a firm understanding of how much control we shall have over the manuscript and how much our subject will be able to decide what she'll say and *how* she'll say it. We'll need to be firm; she's the authority and will supply the facts and opinions; we're the writer and will determine the style. People, even celebrities, being what they are, agreement may not be possible and we may have to call it quits. To protect ourselves, we spell it out at the beginning and include a clause in our contract so that if we ever come to separation, she keeps the unfinished manuscript to do with what she will and we receive a stated payment to cover our time and work.

With luck, such a contretemps will never occur. Many partnerships of all kinds fall apart, but many succeed and, if both parties are agreed that they want to see the project completed and will share in the proceeds, a happy conclusion is probable. The promise of seeing one's name in print and receiving public affirmation of one's success in a career is a powerful incentive to behave like a nice little collaborator.

Surely, one would think, the number of people we could approach with such an idea must be very small. *Au contraire, mes amis.* The woods are full of "experts" on this and "authorities" on that. Note that the "with-writers" I have referred to chose psychologists and psychotherapists as their writing partners and wrote about health and diet and family affairs. If we look around us we'll find juvenile court judges, family doctors, insurance company presidents even, whose name would look mighty good on books or articles giving good advice on family problems. There's always a young new audience for life stories of athletes, successful business executives, criminal prosecutors (or criminals), women's rights advocates, and veteran politicians. And in every community, there are some eminent people whose eminence consists solely of having lived so long. Their *pioneer days* are potential sellers if recounted with the help of a talented writer.

In the country, there are agronomists whose books or articles about husbandry would be welcomed and successful cattle breeders and chicken raisers to pass on their secrets of success to their successors. There are men and women who are marvelous inventive cooks but couldn't write a readable cookbook to save their lives. And there are hobbyists beyond count who'd love to see their names in print as they tell readers how to play chess or weave wool for a blanket. You name it, and somebody's got it—it's a case of finding someone who has already been *recognized* and has a saleable name.

Some of these may be good only for limited editions, or for small magazines. (By *limited*, I mean an edition of maybe one or two thousand copies, and by *small* I mean one of the publications with editorial content restricted to one or two subjects, like *Boating*, or *North American Quilting*. (There's not much money there for either collaborator, but for the big-time author, there's glory and wider recognition, and for us small-timers, there could be a few pennies plus, more importantly, our name on the cover, listing in publication directories and library catalogues, and proof that we've been published.

Finally, there are among our collaboration prospects some, at least, who will be thrilled at the prospect of having a book of their own. They're willing to pay the initial cost to have it privately printed and trust that part of their investment may come back in the form of sales. Dangerous thinking, perhaps, but who knows? It has happened.

Unless these pay-it-yourself personalities are very wealthy, like an ex-chairman of the board of an international conglomerate or the president of a national bank, they're not likely to go along with a proposal that involves either a very large cash outlay or a big fee for us. All they need to know is that a small but respectable volume can be printed and published for less than the cost of a portrait of themselves in oils, and that our fee will be modest, contingent upon our sharing the profits if such should materialize.

If we can get publisher responses to two or three shared-credit books (making sure that our share of the credit is not so small that no one will be able to read it!) and they are even reasonably successful, we may be sufficiently well established to go for the next one on our own. We may not be famous or infamous but we're a published author and by this time may even be on a first-name basis with an editor. We may even be one of the ghosts who come out of the fog and write our own name in flaming letters across the front jacket of our very own book.

We could be happy with that until some really famous person comes to us and says, "Would you be interested in helping me write a book about my years in television? I could do it myself, you know, but I want to take it easy, and I like your style."

Could we ever turn it down?

All "with" books, of course, needn't have a famous name, although the books I'm thinking of now had perhaps better be called "and" books instead. We have a friend, or a cousin, or even a friendly spouse who shares our interest in becoming a writer. Perhaps we could have a go at it together. We're both retired, so (theoretically, at least) we have leisure time as well as a lifetime of experiences to share. We go to a writing class together, go fifty-fifty on a correspondence course or a library of how-to books about writing.

Perhaps he or she is good at research and not so good at writing, or has the imagination while we're strong on facts. Some writers find conversation difficult and could benefit from having a talking-in-print expert alongside; others make a botch at characterizations or descriptions. So two heads and two sets of hands and feet are better than one. We arrange a series of "editorial conferences," put on the coffeepot and begin churning up a plot. We either put our whole conversation on a tape for revising later or one of us makes detailed notes.

What we produce, if we ever do produce anything, will go off to a publisher labeled "By Us *and* Her"—we'll split the glory and divide the cash, again according to a contract we've both signed at the outset. (Even if we're the best of friends, there's always the possibility that those who start as the best of friends may end up as the worst of enemies, particularly if the joint venture is a smashing success and they argue over who gets what, or a dismal flop and each blames the other for ruining his or her career.)

The best kind of "and" collaborations are those between spouses or friends with different but complementary talents. Women writers and men photographers go well together, or the man who writes and the woman who sketches. That doesn't mean all togetherness books must cross gender lines. Nordoff and Hall (two men) wrote *Mutiny on the Bounty*, and there have been many other all-male or all-female teams that have written popular novels, nonfiction and plays.

Writing together can be fun, particularly for older people who miss the regular companionship of fellow workers during their "active" years. It provides an excuse for getting out, or having someone else come in. It helps us keep from becoming so self centered that we never think or talk of anything but ourselves. And when it comes to looking for markets, having two writer-salespersons on the road instead of one may be a distinct advantage.

"With" writer or "and" writer, there's something there for us old-timers to think about.

THE INVISIBLE BY-LINE
And now for those nearly invisible ghosts who write other people's books, articles, speeches—even, sometimes, their letters—and who never let their own names be known. Great books may be written under others' names, but the ghost remains anonymous, reaping none of the glory and, of course, sharing none of the blame if book, speech, or article is a bust.

Unknown writers seldom become true ghosts because ghost writers, unlike "with" writers or collaborators, are sought either by the persons wishing to be "ghosted" or by the publisher who wants the Big Man's or Big Woman's story but also wants it to be readable as well as authentic. We don't go after them: If we're well known, they come after us.

If we're willing to accept anonymity, our raison d'etre for ghost writing can only be money. How much is the nominal author of the piece in question or its publisher prepared to pay, and on what terms? We should ask for a substantial fee, at least half payable in advance and the balance on delivery of the completed manuscript. Our contract should stipulate that if, at any time prior to the completion of the manuscript, it should be rejected by subject or publisher, we must be fully compensated for the work we have put into it. There must also be a stated limitation to the amount of editorial revision that can be demanded without additional compensation. If these terms seem unduly prejudiced in the ghost's favor, well, that's why ghost-seekers go to well-known writers instead of taking a chance on unproved authors. The ghost-seekers want a professional, and professionals know how to protect themselves from working for nothing.

"MY FELLOW AMERICANS . . ."
Speech writing is a more promising form of ghosting for the part-time writer. Political parties, national organizations, and big

companies that have public relations departments normally have speech writers on their staffs and only occasionally call for outside help. But there are opportunities for free-lancers who will take the time to work on, and with, a potential client who has no support system.

Local politicians constitute the best potential market for our speech-writing talent. Candidates for local office and those seeking election to state and national legislatures are often poor at planning and organizing speeches—and sometimes poor speakers as well. They need help and are not considered important enough to receive individual assistance from the party's professional writers.

Our best approach is made through the organization of the party we support—if we're Democrats, we'll obviously write better speeches for Democratic candidates. Similarly, if we're dog lovers, we'll be effective speech writers for humane society campaigners or municipal dogcatchers. Being active in the party will be a help at developing contacts, although it may also cause our prospective mouthpiece to ask us to work for the cause as well as write for it—which means, for free. But even that would be a beginning.

Having been engaged as speech writers, we should take every opportunity to listen to our partner speak, or even just converse. We should note words and sentence constructions he or she has difficulty handling, study whether short or long sentences seem to work better, heed carefully his or her familiarity with popular expressions, professional jargon, or humor, to make the speech comfortable to say and convincing to hear.

For fifteen years in the forties and fifties, I wrote every speech delivered by one of the Canadian members of Parliament and the Canadian Senate. At the beginning, he would rough out the kind of speech he wanted to deliver, what he wanted to say, and how he would say it. I would take that and put it in speech form. Later, I became so familiar with his mannerisms and so aware of his policies that he would simply call me and say, "Can you send me a fifty-minute talk on pest control?" In twenty-four hours, he'd have it. He made a great many speeches, not only in Parliament, but to clubs and organizations across Canada. I not only wrote his speeches: I went and listened to them. When I sat down to write a speech for him, I could *hear* him delivering it.

That's what we must do to be successful speech writers: know and understand what our subject wants to say and then listen in our minds to him or her saying it. And this applies not only to writing for politicians but to preparing speeches for business executives, sales managers, or professional people who are once in a while called to the platform. Unaccustomed as they may be to public speaking, we can make them more comfortable and effective by giving them the proper lines.

A MODERN-DAY CYRANO?

Another rather esoteric and disappearing field for ghosts is letter writing. Readers of the chronicles of nineteenth century immigrants to America will recall many references to scholars who made a business of writing letters for their unschooled compatriots. Today, with universal compulsory education, there are few people who cannot write at least some kind of letter, so the personal writing profession has largely gone. But even in the time since Cyrano de Bergerac's love letter-writing days, there is still a demand not merely for literacy, but for style. Political parties, charitable foundations, fund-raisers of all kinds, direct mail sales organizations, clubs, churches, and various other associations still depend heavily on effective letter writers. Since they're not writing just for fun, these organizations are prepared to pay someone to write the kinds of letters that get action. Besides approaching these organizations individually with sample letters or even complete direct mail campaigns, we should contact local advertising agencies and public relations bureaus. They hire letter writers for their corresponding clients.

Overall, the ghost writing technique is basically the same as that of collaboration. We follow the same interviewing procedures, look for the same documents, press clippings, and records of achievement. The difference is that, when the piece is done and delivered, we fold our tents and silently sneak away, clutching a pay check but nothing more. If we go to the book autographing party, we go as guests or observers and watch the "author" sign copies of our creation. If we watch a televised speech or listen to a "Meet the Author" program on radio, again he/she is there and we never get a mention.

That's what happens to ghosts.

NINE

Marco Polo Slept Here

Much have I travelled in the realms of gold
And many goodly states and kingdoms seen . . .

John Keats ("On First Looking into
Chapman's Homer")

The time has come for us to listen to the siren call of the Far East, to haul out the travel books and the airline schedules, to discover America or visit the old countries in Europe. That's something else we always wanted to do but never had the time, just like the story we wanted to write but could never finish!

When we retire, we said, we're going to TRAVEL. We'd like to write, too. No reason why we shouldn't do both. Traveling and writing, like ham and eggs, go together. Marco Polo did it. So did a host of professional writers. We could become one of them, off to see a bullfight in Spain, to "watch the dawn come up like thunder out of China 'cross the bay," or ride with a white-robed Arab sheik across the desert, and home again to write it all down.

Hold on a minute. Before we get too excited about this fascinating new career and start packing our bags and getting our passports, there are three conditions we should keep in mind.

First: We must be able to write well, better than the copywriters do in the travel booklets and folders distributed by the tourist agencies and transportation companies. And copywriters aren't all that bad.

Second: We must forget about the Taj Mahal and the Acropolis, the Great Wall of China, or the Tower of London. You may not believe it, but they've all been "done" before, not once but many hundreds of times. Better writers than we have given these choice tourist sites a going over. We need to find a place that nobody else has written about, or that has been described by so few that there are many possible new approaches, or angles, to another story. Sounds difficult, but there's still an awful lot of world out there till somebody comes along and blows it all up.

And third: The place we choose must be unusual, off the beaten track, fascinating, breathtaking, or some other adjective, and better yet, reachable by an existing transportation facility—that is, by train, plane, boat, or car. Unusual places that are accessible only to travelers arriving by balloon or rocket are not particularly appealing to most travel page editors.

Travel may be romantic, educational, and all that, but descriptions of unusual but inaccessible places are of limited appeal to travel page editors. Unlike the exotic scenes displayed in almost any issue of *National Geographic*, what's shown in travel sections is intended to attract tourists who actually want to visit. Travel pages are supported by advertising from transportation companies, tourist bureaus, and hotels. Little of that is likely to be attracted by articles about places where nobody goes.

DOES OUR WRITING NEED A TUNE-UP?

The first condition is entirely up to us. If writing as more than a hobby is a new occupation for us, then we should (I'd almost say *must*) agree to be educated, if only to learn the factors that influence editorial decisions. We don't need to take a course in short story writing or dramatic criticism to learn to write travel articles; we do need to know what editors look for in the way of descriptions, history, personal observations, etc. We'll probably be best served if we can find an instructor who'll give us individual or small group instruction concentrating on this form of descriptive writing.

Whatever our taste in reading has been, it's vitally important that we concentrate on reading contemporary travel books—either tourist guidebooks or travel adventure, depending on the type of book or article we contemplate writing.

The second condition, that we stay away from the commonplace, or use such tourist magnets simply as jumping-off places on the way to our ultimate goals, is simple enough. If we go through a six months' supply of travel pages from any of the large metropolitan newspapers, peruse a few copies of *National Geographic* and the *Diner's Club* and *American Express* magazines, we will see what and where the popular travel spots are. What the articles don't tell us, the advertisements will. These are all places we might like to visit, and we can do so en route, but they are not likely to yield the kind of stories or articles we're going to be able to sell.

We get there first, then use our imagination and initiative. How do we find the unknown? When V. Tony Hauser, the wandering photographer, wanted to find new places and strange faces to photograph, he went to the most remote section of Mexico, climbed what many people thought was too difficult a mountain path, and came upon a Mayan village where no one spoke English or Spanish and where life went on as it had for a thousand years. He came down with a carrying case full of exposed film which was the material for exhibitions in galleries and museums in the United States and Canada, and reviews in national and international photo magazines.

That's what we do. Find, if not an inaccessible mountain, a path that is not well worn. And we find it because very near most well-known and oft-visited places there is a village, a lake, a mountain—a unique attraction well known to local residents but never the centerpiece of a travel article or book. There are hundreds of such places in the United States alone, just waiting for someone to discover them.

A footloose writer many years ago got the idea there were a lot of good little inns in New England (and the Carolinas), took time out to visit them one by one and came up with a book. Title, *New England Inns*. (What else?) Readers were introduced to little hostels in towns and villages, sometimes only a few miles away from where they lived. Many of these inns had long and interesting histories; some served extraordinarily good food; others were located in the midst of scenic wonders.

ROOM AT THE INN
It wasn't long before *Inns of Here* and *Inns of There* books were popping out of publishers' offices all over but, I assure you, there's still room for another "inns" book or series of articles. There are innkeepers in many states who are longing for and deserving of recognition. Perhaps their buildings will not be reeking of history or loaded with quaint architecture, but they'll be places where off-the-beaten-path travelers stay and where some gentle innkeeper and spouse have provided something typically American

for the blasé traveler. Someone must go looking for them.

Before launching our inn-writing project, unless we're doing it for fun and the possible hope of selling it later, we'll have to go back to our marketing chores and line up a potential publisher. Finding the inns won't be difficult: Tourist bureaus will give us lists of "approved" inns and hotels in various state regions; motor clubs and travel agents will help us map out a tour route and even make reservations for us if we wish. Locating a publisher may not be quite that easy. *Books in Print*, available for examination in the reference section of public libraries, will have a list of inn books and their publishers. This will give us an idea of what areas have been covered as well as a list of publishers who might be interested in another venture in a field with which they're already familiar. Those who publish travel books not specifically connected to inns should also be noted in our journal's section on publishers' addresses.

While in the library, why not check the shelves for books about inns or hotels, borrow those that look interesting, and read them? Then trot off to one or two local bookstores, see what they have among their travel books, and note publishers' names and publication dates. Maybe even buy one or two; they'll be a good investment.

Armed with a list of potential publishers, we will make up a brief outline of what we propose to do and prepare what's known in the business world as a sales presentation. We describe, first, the territory we plan to cover: a single state, a group of Midwest, Eastern, or Pacific coast states, or Canadian provinces. Then we present a tentative list of the inns we will visit, and add a paragraph or two outlining the form and style that our descriptions of the places will take. An editor will wish to know something about us, our credentials, whether we have written anything else, and what all this traveling is going to cost (cost the publisher, that is, not us). That information goes in a covering letter.

Let's check to see if there's a local publisher or two in the area we're going to visit. They might never have published an inn-book before but might be interested because ours would be local. Now we decide whether to send out three or four submissions at once or take them one at a time. I'd favor a multiple submission, but I'd make sure I tell those I write to that they're one of four on my list.

If we have a publisher who has expressed any interest (and it's by no means impossible to find one who likes books that stay around a long time, selling perhaps only a few hundred copies a year) the innkeepers are likely to welcome us with open arms, a room overlooking the main scenic attraction, and meals they'd love to serve to a New York restaurant critic. It could be a nice little two month holiday for a retired couple and could produce new friends and tips on future vacation spots to visit as well as a profitable book.

That's easy traveling, light on the pocketbook, and has reasonable prospects for at least a partial cash return. We can make the whole trip in our own car, on buses or by train. We don't have to worry about customs, language, or the drinking water (although one favorite-inns writer I know reported that the drinking water in an inn she visited was so heavy with sulphur—it came from a natural spring out back—she could almost chew it. And the smell!) By and large, however, we're not likely to encounter any food or water problems that will require medical attention if we confine our explorations to our own country.

COME TO THE FAIR

That's only scratching the surface of the country market. There are countless county fairs, far more than you or I can imagine. Many of them have unique local features but have never been "written up" beyond the columns of the county weeklies. Many of them have attractions that are worth describing. Or perhaps some travel-minded retirees wouldn't mind carting their portable typewriters back and forth across the continent to come up with *North America's Best County Fairs.*

What's so different about fairs? Seen one and you've seen them all, haven't you? Nope. The only resemblance between a county fair in Texas and one in New Hampshire or Wisconsin is that in all three there are likely to be a lot of cows wandering about. In one state they're lassoing them, in another they're milking them. Each fair has its specialty, its own local color, and its own traditions. They can be rated good, bad, or indifferent, and some Senior writer who can probably remember what fairs were like in the thirties should do the rating.

Start with county fairs and where do you go next year? Quilting

bees, maple sugar run-offs, berry-picking festivals, country auc-
tions, antique shows, frog-jumping contests—the list goes on and
on. Good old-fashioned Americans are just as good subjects for
travel writers as any tribe of dancing dervishes or Peruvian llama
hunters.

But, we Seniors with long-developed wanderlust say, that's
just the nitty-gritty stuff. We yearn more for the exotic and the romantic, want to wake up in the morning listening to the parrots
squawk deep in the African jungle. So we head for distant climes,
armed with guidebooks and other writers' travel books that tell
us what territories have been covered and what other articles and
books have already been written.

We pick a more civilized location to start, heading instead for a
country with indoor plumbing—say, Greece. How much more
civilized could we get? And how much more commonplace, for a
writer? We don't plan to stay there long, however. Instead, we
start making inquiries at the Greek tourist office, at our hotel information desk, anywhere we meet Greek people. We tell them
we're looking for off-beat places outside the mainstream, away
from the big tourist centers—someplace where they've never
heard of McDonald's.

Greeks, like the French, Germans, or Australians, have been
taught to like tourists, who bring that most delightful of all
gifts—money. When we say we want to do an article or a book
about some fresh, unpublicized town or lake or region in their
country, they are normally delighted to be of assistance. They
may not be able to give us exactly what we want but they can
point us in the right direction and, just as at home we have to find
county fairs or country inns that are different, we must search for
the potential tourist attractions that have so far been tourist-free.

We scour the countryside, riding on buses, in rented cars, maybe on donkey-back; we observe, we drink, we meet people, and
maybe climb a mountain or two. The people we meet are different; they play games we have never seen, like hockey with two
sticks and a stone; they have distinctive regional dances and costumes and often lots of local folklore. And, to a Greek, folklore
means not what his grandfather did but what his forebears did a
thousand years ago.

We go back home with an article or a book on *Where Only*

Greek Meets Greek, and probably start a stampede of travel writers and tourists to those once isolated retreats.

THE WELL-TRAVELED TRAVEL PIECE

Perhaps the newspaper travel editors and book publishers are not all that interested in our new discovery. The community paper might be and, as a last resort, we might give it to them; but the compensation will be small—$25 or $50 at most, hardly enough to pay for a winter in Greece. So was it all wasted time and effort? Not necessarily. Check out other markets. Airlines publish in-flight magazines; and in-flight magazine editors like articles that can give readers another reason for going back to Greece. Some airline publications pay very well for articles and photographs; others will offer free transportation and, sometimes, hotel accommodations. So, at worst, we have a cheap vacation and the editors won't object if we sell the article to another magazine as well.

Keep on looking for outlets, as diligently as we looked for the overlooked Garden of Eden, and we'll be astonished to discover how many "little magazines" there are in America that actually pay good money for well-written travel articles. Some of these are right here in our hometown and are overlooked completely by the big name travel writers, leaving the field wide open for small fry like us.

In every big city, and in some medium-sized or even small ones, there are professionally produced, free-distribution magazines that report on local restaurants, theaters, business and social activities for residents who live in affluent neighborhoods. They also have articles on international fashion and international travel, because these subjects attract national advertising. Some of these publications are entirely staff-written, some are poor excuses for trapping advertising dollars. But to survive and do well in the highly competitive magazine field, neighborhood publications must be more than just printed pages bound together with a pretty cover. The best of them are as good as, and sometimes better than, their paid-circulation competitors. Add to these the number of special interest magazines distributed regionally or nationally to homes in selected residential areas, and we have a sizable number of travel article prospects that we may not even find listed in periodical directories.

In the city where I live, I receive every month a glossy magazine called *Calendar* which I'd gladly buy if it didn't come to me free; a seventy- or eighty-page publication called *City Woman* which is aimed at career women but which I snatch from my wife to find out what the other sex is doing and where it's going; a men's magazine called *Quest*, which my wife snatches from me because it has better articles in it than the commercially published nonfiction magazine for which we pay $20 a year; a business-oriented quarterly called *Economic Affairs* that talks about money, and which we snatch from each other. All these arrive in addition to three weekly newspapers, *The Westmount Examiner*, the *Suburban*, and *Downtowner*. Every one of these periodicals at some time or another carries articles about travel to far-off places.

Admittedly, they can get these articles free from government tourist bureaus, transportation companies, and travel agencies. And some of those we see obviously come from those sources. But there's been a big change in the freebie publication world in the last two decades. They've improved in content, appearance, and style. They pay more for what they publish and they get paid more for advertising.

That means contracting out to free-lancers for at least a few travel articles a year. We should give them a chance to contract with us. They won't pay *National Geographic* rates but, with all due respect to our rare writing talents, they won't be getting *National Geographic* copy. And they can be helpful to us in other ways. An airline or shipping company or railroad that might not be eager to help us along our way might respond to an appeal from one of the better free-distribution magazines which was sending a writer off on a trip in their territory to do some travel reporting

When we've talked to these city magazine editors, our quest isn't necessarily over. Sitting there, just over the horizon, are a multitude of hotel and restaurant magazines published by the big chains like Hilton, Sheraton and Holiday Inn, or by individual hotels. I edited a Hilton magazine for almost ten years, as a freelance editor, and during that time *bought* travel articles from a dozen different competent but unknown travel writers. We sometimes accepted transportation passes from an advertiser in exchange for ad space, paying our writers with the passes and some cash. None of those who did travel writing for us got rich in the process, but they all got bread and butter money and a chance to see other parts of the world. One of them, now in her late seventies, continues to appear with a by-line over a travel piece in a magazine or newspaper.

Critics say writers live isolated, inner-directed lives, marooning themselves behind a typewriter in an upstairs room or basement den, their only friends the typing apparatus and a standard dictionary. It's not really true for any writer; no one can write well in a vacuum. Writing is about people and things and places and events, and if we keep ourselves apart from the world, we soon won't have much to write about.

It's particularly not true about travel writers. Not only must we go places and meet people and share experiences, we must also become marketing experts and sales people, calling on editors, airlines, tourist officials, hotel and restaurant owners. Am I going too far when I say "restaurant owners"? One large, popular restaurant I know of personally hires a free-lance writer three or four times a year to write a regional travel piece for its menu—one of those big, hard-to-handle and harder-to-read-in-the-dark preludes to dining that get handed out in the flossier eating places. The article changes with the season, emphasizing local fishing areas in the spring and skiing territories in the winter. For the history buff-diner, it includes special pieces on notable regional historic sites. It does about everything except inform its readers about other good places to dine.

The menus are so interesting, customers ask for copies to take home. At first, the owner complied; now he charges two dollars a copy. He also pays more for his articles, finding very few quality free-lancers willing to produce in exchange for free meals.

A GUIDEBOOK TO OUR OWN HOMETOWN

Opportunities are constantly beckoning to the Senior writer who has time, is free to travel, and doesn't need to command even a living wage for his or her work. Just as there are still hundreds of neighborhoods, streets, apartment complexes, and retirement villages that don't have a community newspaper and would welcome one if we published it, so there are hundreds of regions and communities that don't have an attractive, well-written and pleasantly illustrated *saleable* guide book or history. There are books without end about cities like Boston, New York, Los Angeles, or Toronto, but very few popular books about ramblings in a neighborhood, or tours of city gardens, like *Days and Nights in the Back Bay, Strolling Through Old World Brooklyn*, or *Flora and Fauna in Toronto's Glens*.

If we visit Cape Cod or the Florida Gold Coast we'll be offered picture postcards, aptly named throw-away guides to local restaurants and historic sites and only an occasional small book, written from the heart, about a winding street of old homes, an old decaying port that once sheltered sailing ships from around the world, or neighborhood legends.

There are such books—quite a few of them—but more could be written and bought and treasured by the people who live there and the tourists who visit. They needn't be expensive, hard-cover volumes; they don't even need to be long. A hundred pages or so with illustrations is enough for the reader on the run. Attractively printed (no cheap paper or lousy illustrations will do), they may become miniature table-toppers, kept on display by residents proud of their community and happy to belong to it, or treasured as mementos of a period in their lives before they moved away to greener pastures.

A neighbor of ours who has moved a lot—nineteen times in fifty years—says that every time her family bought a house in a new area, the first thing they did was search the libraries and bookstores for books that would tell them about their new community. Sometimes they were lucky: a house next door, or the street they lived on, had some wonderful antecedents. Only once did they manage to get an authentic historic house of their own and find it mentioned in a rare old book. The best they could do was to have the page photographed and carry the picture about with them as they moved from town to town and country to country.

Almost any community of any size lends itself to a lovingly written hometown travel book, and who can better write it than a Senior Citizen who has lived there for decades? We are the only ones who know for sure whose store stood on the busy midtown corner in the twenties before the big Five and Ten moved in. We know, because we were there and saw it; and we saw it come down. We saw the first street paved and the first elms fall.

A local printer could be interested in a joint publishing venture, or an important local company seeking identification with the community might be willing to sponsor such a book and ask only for acknowledgement or credit on the title page.

I'm one of those people who hate to spend a vacation (even at home) looking at the sand, staring at the sea, or sitting in the park watching the children at play. I hate visiting cold churches and old cathedrals and am not a bit keen about walking about in art galleries and museums. I like best of all to have something to do, and that means, nine times out of ten, having something to write about. For me, that's travelin', whether it's around the block or around the globe.

For some of us, the best travel writing comes from traveling with someone. Fortunately even the best travel articles or books go better with pictures, so if we have a spouse or a friend or neighbor who likes traveling and can handle either a camera or sketchpad, we've got the promise of companionship and creative cooperation. If we're not so lucky, then we should buy our own camera, take a few lessons on how to use it and become at least a fair photo-journalist.

"R-Day" (R means Retirement) has dawned. If we haven't done it already, we start now planning a new kind of future. Because we have always said, "The day we retire, we start seeing the world," and because we're also determined to get at that writing, we take a couple of days off to celebrate and then begin charting our new course. For the first time in our lives, the world is our oyster. We can go where we like, write what we like. Move over, Marco Polo: a new world traveling author is on the way.

TEN

How to Enjoy Books, Theater, and the Movies—for Free!

Reviewers are usually people who would have been poets, historians, biographers, etc., if they could; they have tried their talents at one or the other and have failed; therefore they turn critics.

Samuel Taylor Coleridge, in a lecture on Shakespeare and Milton

One shouldn't always argue with the authority one quotes at the beginning of a chapter, but sometimes they are so outrageously wrong, it's difficult to resist the temptation. One can sense more than a little pique in Coleridge's rather snide remarks about reviewers. Is it possible some nineteenth century critic was a little less than ecstatic about the learned poet's *Ancient Mariner*, or was the poet just seeking attention by coining a two-liner before a captive audience? Chances are we'll never know, but since Coleridge's time, and I suspect before, there have been a number of highly respected reviewers who could not only write poetry, history, or biographies very well but often did so.

A less harsh judgment and one that would be closer to the mark might be: Many would-be poets, historians, or biographers have undisputed writing talents but were unable, for one reason or another, to find a market for them. They might well turn to reviewing the works of others less talented in order to earn a living. I can't see anything particularly wrong with that.

Before we get completely off the subject of community newspapers and magazines, however, let's forget about Coleridge and review the enticing prospects these regional publications offer for enlarging our personal libraries, enlivening our winter evenings and extending our cultural horizons—all for free. And just perhaps for treating us to snack suppers or paying part of our rent, as well.

In case you haven't guessed it by now, I'm talking about linking the two—the community press and book, theater, and movie reviewing—to make us *reviewers*, not *critics*, which are something else again. We can be purveyors of news about what new books are on the shelves, what new plays on stage, and what new pictures on the screen. There could be no more pleasant occupation for retired teachers, professors, or men and women who worked in the professions or were associated with the world of entertainment.

There is space available—and limited amounts of money—for well-written reviews in many of the community publications we have been talking about. In many cases, the only reason that space remains unfilled is that no one has approached the editor with an offer to fill it with worthwhile copy at moderate or no cost. If we feel confident that we could supply the missing ingredient, we may approach the editor with two strong selling points:

1. In any residential community where a local publication is considered viable, there will be an audience for information about books, the stage, and screen. A timely, intelligent review column will therefore be serving a useful purpose and enhancing the value of the publication to its readers.

2. Book publishers, shops, and theaters aren't big advertisers in community papers like supermarkets, *but* a paper that publishes articles of interest to people who buy books or go to theaters has a readership that interests book publishers, shops, and theaters, and consequently they might become small but regular and, more important, *new* advertisers. We should tell the editor that.

GETTING FREEBIES

Having convinced the editor or publisher that we can help make the publication more interesting to local readers, we can then explain what he or she must do to help us do our part. We can't be expected to buy books, or run to the library to borrow them, in order to write a review; nor can we be asked to pay for admission to theaters to see plays or movies we want to tell our readers about. But no publisher or theater owner is going to give us books or theater tickets just because we ask for them.

If the editor asks, that's different. Obviously, the *Sunnydale Gazette*, circulation fifteen hundred copies, is not going to publish an equivalent of the sixty-page *New York Times Review of Books*. The space available per issue for book reviews may be as little as a single column, tabloid-size, or a single page in a standard 8½ x 11 magazine page. Believe me, that's more, proportionately, than the *Times* allows in its regular editions. It's enough for a review of one book with a strong local interest, by a local author, perhaps, or about a local subject; two or three short reviews of special interest books or talked-about best sellers. At Christmas and other gift seasons, a roundup of suitable books with four- or five-line comments would have reader and advertiser interest.

We are the reviewers and, before we go to talk to the editor, we should have in mind the kind of column we want to write and the type of books we want to review. Book publishers, we know, are funny people. For the big papers, they ship copies of everything they publish, keep their fingers crossed and hope that at least half of them get mentioned. It's costly but they can't afford to miss the chance that a single review by a prestigious reviewer in a prestige publication might start the ball rolling and transform a slow-selling dog into a best-selling lion.

When it comes to doling out books to small publications, they don't. They wait until one of them asks for a book by title, almost guarantees a review and promises to send them a copy of the review when it appears. They are not about to ship four or five books a week to our little Sunnydale paper, which couldn't possibly spare the space for them. Even when asked, they won't always comply; to stay solvent, publishers have to be a little bit niggardly about handing out samples at $25 or $30 a crack, and the Sunnydale market, after all, is not that big.

Later on, when we're established reviewers and the publishers know us by name and may sometimes even suggest a title we would be interested in, we can make our requests directly. Meanwhile, we're better off to let the *Gazette* editor do it, though we could write the letter for him. How do we know what books we want or, more importantly, what books our potential readers might want? We subscribe to magazines like *Publishers Weekly* (or *Quill and Quire* in Canada). In them we get publishers' advance notices of books. We read the notices carefully, also check

PW reports on book sales, select a title here and a title there, always with local interest in mind. It need not be by a local or regional author or about a specific local subject. It could be about sailing, for instance, if we live by a lake or in a seaport; or a historical novel about the Civil War if there is a Blue and Grey battlefield nearby.

Once books are received, we do our best to write reviews that will interest our readers and attract publishers' attention. If we turn out to be pretty good at it, next thing we know we'll get publishers' invitations to book launchings, get to meet the people who write the books we review and sometimes, when a book comes out with a reference to our town or area, we might even be asked by a big city publication to contribute a review for them. Wonder of wonders, that could produce a check with three figures!

Publishers—and even more so their authors who are often starved for recognition—read reviews, no matter how small or unimportant the source. It's not entirely a matter of ego, though that plays a part, and all of us who write are entitled to some of that. Authors like to know what people out there think of their work, even if they may have to read it in a mimeographed church newsletter. (And that, by the way, is another place a would-be reviewer may find a first testing ground. Church papers have a place for book reviews, sometimes with a social rather than a religious viewpoint; a series of well-written reviews in one of these limited-circulation publications may some day find itself on the lap of a churchgoing editor who could spot a hidden talent.)

Somebody once asked a great American marketing expert what single medium was responsible for the sale of his product. He replied he could not name any one; it could be an article in a newspaper, an advertisement in a national magazine, a billboard display, a radio or TV commercial or the little give-away fliers a supermarket chain stuffed in its grocery bags. One shouldn't compare writers to canned soups or chocolate bars, but they, too, can find themselves famous because somebody important spotted their name on top of a book review in a nondescript paper. In other words, we should never overlook the importance of the unimportant—it could turn out to be the most important thing in our lives.

That's enough about getting to be a book reviewer. Suppose we don't like reading books but we love going to the theater or the movies. What we do now is even simpler than writing a letter to a publisher. Armed with an introduction from our editor, we go to the managers of local theaters and movie houses, explain that we'd like to review their shows for our Sunnydale weekly and request a pair of first-night passes so that we may look at what we want to review. If only because we have grey or white manes, the manager will realize we're not some kid looking for a free outing, and he may agree to give us a try with his next show. We needn't insist on that first-night bit; second night could be just as good if we're writing for a weekly or a monthly magazine. We do need good seats, however, and shouldn't be shunted off into the last row corner seats.

It's important that our editors fulfill their agreements to send copies of our reviews to book publishers and theater managers even if our clever comments are not all that effusive. As President Roosevelt used to say: "All publicity is good publicity; even bad publicity." Publishers and play or movie producers usually feel the same way though there have been cases of well-known critics being barred from theaters by angry producers, and publishers are sometimes unwilling to send free copies of their books to those reviewers who consistently tear them to shreds. In the long run, of course, it's the theater producer or publisher who suffers, because books and plays need exposure. Look what happened to *Abie's Irish Rose;* we Seniors can remember that one even if it's ancient theater lore to our Juniors. Critics unanimously panned it, but they did so in large space and catchy if nasty headlines. So it played for seven years, one of the longest runs in Broadway history.

THE DISCERNING REVIEWER

Reviewing, much as it may be scorned by some defensive professional writers, is a legitimate art. To be good at it, one must have some special knowledge and the ability to discern the difference between quality and trash. And just as a fiction writer must learn *how* to write novels or short stories, and a poet to write poetry, we who seek to review the works of writers and playwrights and actors must study the basics of *how* it is done. A genuine interest in the subject of a book and the style of its writer is essential, as are a knowledge and understanding of what makes a good play or a good actor.

We can't successfully review books or plays or movies if we haven't an idea about how books are written or what constitutes good drama or fine acting. And we'd be quite out of our depth if, for instance, we were to try to review a book by Carl Sagan about the history of the human brain if all our experience had been in selling real estate or shoes or in cooking family dinners.

If knowledge of the subject is important, a degree of reviewing "know-how" is equally so. How does one write a review? What is the difference between review and criticism? "It's much easier to be critical than correct," Benjamin Disraeli once remarked when he was prime minister of England. He also wrote novels. And Henry James, the nineteenth century expatriate American novelist, said, "The practice of 'reviewing' in general has nothing in common with the art of criticism."

As Senior Citizens, with a world of experience behind us, we are particularly suited to be reviewers; few are qualified to be critics, although the latter skill may appear to be the more desirable. We've watched best sellers rise and fall and are often amazed at the changes in our own taste for reading or movie viewing. We've seen once-popular plays tossed in the trash can or laughed off the stage, and we've wondered at those that have survived to be as popular as ever in this technological age. Television programs have introduced us to writers, performers, reviewers, and critics so that we are better informed about what goes on in editorial offices and backstage than we were in our prime. This all makes us good raw material for reviewing but is not enough to allow us to pose as pundits and tell our readers positively what they *should* or *should not* read or see.

It does entitle us to report whether or not we found a book, a play, or a movie dull, agreeable, or fascinating—that is our *opinion*, not a criticism. As reviewers we wouldn't be serving any real purpose if we didn't have opinions, likes, and dislikes and, above all, good judgment. Expressing those opinions through favorable or unfavorable reviews does not mean we are setting ourselves up as critics. Those exalted creatures know all about, and concern themselves with, the *techniques* of writing and performing, sometimes overlooking entirely the capacity of a book or play to provide enjoyment for people who couldn't care less whether the author or actor "cleverly conceals [his] real meanings in an avalanche of nuances reminiscent of the novels of Nathaniel Hawthorne or a Chekhov drama."

We satisfy ourselves and our generally unsophisticated readership if we simply say whether a book or play was worth the fifteen bucks a copy, or seat—and why or why not—and say it in language all our readers will understand. The most successful restaurant reviewer I know (and there's another field for Senior Citizen reviewers) never uses a French word if an English one will do. For *table d'hôte* she writes *complete meal* and for those tasty little bites the French call *escargots* she substitutes *snails*, right out loud. As book and play reviewers, let us do likewise!

To be successful, all reviewers must have some special talent that makes them interesting and helpful to their readers. Primarily, of course, they must be interested in and enjoy reading books or going to the theater. But as Seniors, we add another dimension. We've been around a long time and have a personal acquaintanceship with the past. We sat at the feet of the Barrymores (on the screen, at least) and read the first struggling books of the Ferbers and the Steinbecks. We witnessed firsthand (not through articles in the scholarly journals) the emergence of a strong, vibrant new literary America, beginning with Hemingway and going on to Norman Mailer, Philip Roth, and a score of powerful women writers who threatened to dominate the fiction market. And we watched moving pictures and plays being transformed from pure entertainment and colorful fantasy into social documentaries and political tracts. We survived through a barrage of propaganda being hurled at us from all sides in print and in sound.

All this should be grist for a mature reviewer's mill.

REVIEWER VS. CRITIC

Every one of us might like to become a *critic* because, as befits people of mature age, we have more or less decided views on everything, including the quality of the books we read and the plays and movies we see, not to mention television, rock music, and the frightening decline in morals of the younger generation. We may also believe we have not only the right but the obligation to pass these opinions on to all those who have not yet had the benefits of our longevity.

These views may be suitable for expression at family gatherings or small neighborhood parties where, for instance, Papa Dan may declaim out loud against "the dirtiest book I ever read" or "that damn play [that] was so nonsensical I wouldn't even take my ten-year-old grandson to see it."

Opinions, true! But genuine literary or dramatic criticism, no! To write a worthwhile *critique* of a book or a play, one must have a far-better-than-average background in English literature or drama. This is not likely to be obtained by many of us if we begin our education after fifty. We could, I suppose, take a four- or five-year course at a university with special classes at theater school or writing seminars. But the exercise, while exciting, might have little practical value since none of the serious, quality publications are potential employers of unknown, seventy-year-old reviewers without reputations, no matter how well-informed they may be.

Fortunately, most community newspapers and city or regional magazines will settle for less. Indeed, they'd be hesitant to employ critics who might easily get them in hot water with potential advertisers and even annoy some of their readers. They'll like us just fine if we do just what reviewers in these publications are supposed to do: present a fair, unbiased account of a performance that will give readers an idea what it's all about.

Now, let's take a look at the three main review categories— books, plays, and movies—and see what their requirements are.

First, the books: Sorry, but it's not enough to say, "I love reading." We're going to be *writers* from now on, not just *readers*. We must find out what constitutes a good review and how one goes about writing it. Part of this we can learn at a writing course or through a correspondence school; it will also be helpful if we study reviews in other publications, not the literary magazines or the newspapers with the big-name critics, but the middle-sized periodicals aiming, much as we will be, at middle-class local audiences.

If the book to be reviewed is fiction, we must be able to give our reader some idea of the plot. Is it a good story? Does it appear gen-

uine or is it unbelievable? Do we find the characters bear any resemblance to living human beings or are they mere dummies or
fantasies? Our readers will want to know where the action takes
place, whether or not it's good entertainment, suitable for the
whole family, if any special knowledge or interest is required in
order to enjoy it, and finally whether it's slow-moving, exciting,
ho-hum, or scary.

If we don't answer those questions, we might as well write:
"Hilary Hicks's new book *The Phantom Fish* (Smith and Smith,
New York, 1983, 198 pages, illustrated, $30) is a sea story that
takes place off Honolulu." Period. That's a "report," sure enough,
and gives our readers the necessary basic information. But it's not
quite enough to satisfy their curiosity either about Hilary Hicks
or the book he probably toiled over for months or years. We could
have written it as easily if we had taken Sidney Smith's advice literally. Away back in 1881, when only a few of the oldest of us
were alive, he wrote: "I never read a book before reviewing it; it
prejudices a man so."

Getting books to review that are beyond our capacity is unlikely since we ourselves are choosing the titles. Let's suppose then
we've asked for a new book about rabbits which has just popped
up on Smith and Smith's spring list. We know something about
them; used to raise them when we were young and lost a small
bundle later on when we invested in a chinchilla farm out in
North Dakota only to have the pesky bunnies break out, dash off
into the woods, and be devoured by coyotes. The book's called
The ABCs of Rabbitry—Angoras, Bunnies and Chinchillas (Get
it?) written by one Peter Hare.

News about the little opus that sells for $19.95 at the bookshop
will fascinate those of our readers who are rabbit raisers or hunters. But how many of them are included in our particular reading
audience? Maybe a hundred. So, to help the kindly publisher who
responded to our request and allowed us to add this tiny volume
to our library (free) and to please the editor who hired us to do his
book review column, we do our best to write a review that will
stress the book's universal appeal.

We begin by looking at the record of the author which, if we're
lucky, will be printed on the back flap of the book jacket. There,
we may find that he has written about stray cats, horses, and Pe-

kinese puppies. Or maybe he's a "famous" novelist who took time out to write about rabbits because he likes them. Anyway, what's on the flap will be in our review and our readers will know that he's not a Johnny-come-lately but an honest-to-goodness professional writer. Here he is, Peter Hare fans, with a brand new book. That's *news*.

We then go on to explain that the subject of the book is rabbits, ignoring the fact that any sane person reading the title would have deduced that information already, and continue with a general description of the book's contents (how to feed rabbits, famous rabbits the author has known, what you can do with rabbits other than just look at them, how to skin them, eat them, play Easter bunny, and how Bugs Bunny became a movie star. It's amazing what you can write about animals that to my mind have no virtues except looking cute.).

We don't need to read and comment on every page or every chapter, though if we asked for the book we're probably interested in it and will be curious about what Mr. Hare has to say. We should give a few interesting quotes and recite maybe three or four incidents to indicate the author's style and treatment of the subject.

Normally, a three- or four-hundred-word review would cover all that most readers would like to know in a book about rabbits—UNLESS the author lives down the street or is married to the daughter of the local Methodist minister. Then the review is not only about the book, it's about the neighbor who wrote it. As a local story, it's worth maybe a whole column or half a page.

For retired teachers, university professors, and professional men and women accustomed to working with words and informing or motivating others, book reviewing should be a comparatively easy art to learn and to practice. But there is room among the small paper reviewers for many Senior Citizens who have no teaching or professional backgrounds but have had years of experience in just living, and have an interest in reading and maybe writing good books. They may find it is not too difficult to review books in which they have a special interest—books about banking reviewed by a retired banker, for example, or a war story reviewed by a World War II veteran. But problems arise when they scan the publishers' lists and don't see anything that has a strong appeal to them. They don't want to let the editor down and miss an issue, but they don't feel equal to tackling a book in which they are not really interested.

Since no one can know everything (though many of us think we do), why not admit our ignorance in this instance and start looking around for fellow retirees who might be interested in forming a semiprofessional reviewer's group, a sort of Sunnydale Round Table like the one at the Algonquin Hotel in the twenties and thirties that hosted a famous coterie of New York critics? We'd all have different tastes and interests, and we could pass the books around so that a story about high life in upper (meaning fifty-two stories and up) Manhattan would land on the lap of a former Madison Avenue advertising executive or fashion model and a crime thriller would go right to that ex-policeman we always said should write his own cops and robbers series.

Such a group would serve a dual purpose. It would provide interesting companionship for retired men and women who find themselves cut off from the stimulating relationships they enjoyed during their active careers, and it would give the review column more authoritative reviews and even wider local appeal. Contact with editors should be the function of one member of the group only, but by-lines would be given to individual members on their printed contributions. And the loot, such as it is, would be fairly distributed.

Working together, we might achieve the objective set out by writer and critic Henry Austin Dobson who recognized the difficulty in having any individual understand everything he was called upon to comment on, and wrote:

> *He praised the thing he understood,*
> *T'were well if every critic would.*

Or shut up and let someone else go to work on it!

CURTAIN GOING UP!

Now, on to the theater: For longtime theater buffs, and there are hundreds of them in every community, anything that keeps them in touch with the performing arts is welcome. And for Seniors with performing or backstage experience or a record of faithful attendance at theatrical performances there is a rewarding editorial niche to be filled in the community press. A former semiprofessional actress I know was for forty years more devoted to the theater than she was to her children or her husband. She performed in many leading parts, dropped back to supporting roles, then directed and produced plays with local amateur companies. Now in her late seventies, she still keeps contact, not only by being in the audience for every new performance, but by sewing buttons on costumes, picking up special props from secondhand stores and antique shops, and listening to young performers learn their lines.

Old actresses never die. Many of them could, if they tried, become theater reviewers or even critics. But they'd need to start reviewing early in their retirement; even community papers are disinclined to engage reviewers who are pushing eighty.

I know that most of us will say that the theater reviewers we all knew about were all great *critics*, not just entertainment page reporters. People like George Jean Nathan and Alexander Woollcott, Dorothy Parker of the old *Vanity Fair*, scourge of the mediocre; Burns Mantle, critic for the *Daily News*, and Brooks Atkinson, who put on a play's final stamp of approval or disapproval for the *Times* were read as much for the way they wrote as for the information they provided. But we're not aiming at the *Times* or the *Daily News* or even at *Woman's Wear Daily*, which, I'm told, prints the best entertainment reviews in North America because it tells its readers (garment buyers visiting New York) what they want to know. We're not aiming at flossy, highbrow criticism that might be used as texts at the Yale Drama School, but down-to-earth reports on whether a show is good, bad, or just lousy, what it's about, who's playing in it, and how hard it is to get tickets.

But we're back here in the suburb of Sunnydale, remember, and if we're very lucky the entertainment editor of the big daily downtown might ask us to do a guest review of a show because he or she read what we wrote in the *Sunnydale Gazette* a while back. Or the regular reviewer for the big city *Current Events Magazine* might be sick or on vacation, or there might be two openings the same night, and we could get a call as backup. Of such *ifs* and *mights* are budding reviewers' dreams composed.

Meanwhile, and until those lucky breaks occur, we should keep clearly in mind the audience we are writing for. Many of our neighbors like to go to the theater and will even settle for seats at an amateur production by students at the local high school or the Sunnydale Little Theater. They go for an evening's enjoyment, not for a lesson on how to become a Shakespearean actor, but before they shell out five bucks for a seat, they'd like to know: (1) Is the show any good, in our opinion? (2) Is it funny or sad? (3) Who's playing in it, someone they know or a visiting "star"? (4) How long does it last? Should they take along a snack, or will it all be over before 10 p.m.? They may also be pleased to know something about facilities for the handicapped, whether the seats are comfortable or not, and if there is adequate parking. (These questions may be considered beyond the scope of a theater review but, believe me, in many cases, they are more important than a description of a prima donna's hat.)

If we're good reviewers, answer all the questions a potential audience may ask, and realize that what we are really doing is just what they taught us at journalism school, we're being good *reporters*. We can also win friends by adding a note or two about the theater acoustics, individual performer's voices and accents, and whether or not the play is easy to follow and comprehend, something all modern plays definitely are not. (Just look at the puzzled expressions of exiting theatergoers when the final curtain rings down.)

It's a decided help if we're one of the past performers. But if we are, we should take care not to be too familiar with the dramatic arts and introduce theatrical jargon understood by players and some theater buffs but a complete mystery to the ordinary people who buy tickets, sit out front, and read our column. An occasional sentence or phrase showing how hip we are to the theater world is permissable but we shouldn't overdo it. In any event, we should try to avoid being self-conscious, sitting there, biting our nails and thinking constantly about the smart things we can say instead of about the smart things that are being said on stage or screen.

Dorothy Parker, another critic who could write, could get away with short reviews like: "*The House Beautiful* was the play lousy," and, "Her acting ran the gamut from A to B." Everybody remembered Miss Parker; nobody remembered the plays. And that is not really the function of a theater reviewer. In fact, E.B. White, the famous newspaper editor who hired and fired critics in his day, thought so little of the critical wisecracker, he wrote:

> *The critic leaves at curtain fall,*
> *To find, in starting to review it,*
> *He scarcely saw the play at all*
> *For watching his reaction to it.*

In the theater today, as in Shakespeare's time, "the play's the thing" and our job will be simply to tell people where it is playing, what it's about, who the players are, and what a seat costs. Nowhere is it suggested that we should tell the performers to move over and let us occupy central stage.

GOLDEN AGER, SILVER SCREEN

At last we come to the movie review. How does it differ from the review of live performances on stage? Well, first, more people go to the movies than to plays, and most movies are designed and produced for the masses and not for the elite. We don't write *down to* but should write for a less informed and less critical audience. People go to the movies for the story (or the sex and/or violence) more than for the performance. There are a few all-out art-film buffs, but they're not for the likes of us, or more correctly, we're not for the likes of them. Unless, of course, we're one of them and have been members of motion picture clubs, make our own movies, or are old film fans. In that case, we should be able to find a paper or magazine that caters to cinema addicts and would appreciate an authoritative column by one of them.

Again with movies, we might find the group idea helpful. We could pass around the tickets and assignments so the adventure fan gets the big war movies, the romanticist the love stories, and the jet setter the drawing room comedies, as they used to be called. Collectively, we could become the bright stars of the *Sunnydale Gazette,* all because we would know and understand what we were writing about.

Mostly, movie review readers today are interested in knowing (1) Is the picture any good? They suspect that every film they see advertised as "the season's biggest hit" is a B movie very thinly disguised. (If there was ever a case of crying wolf once too often, it's in motion picture advertising. If a good movie does come along, there are no adjectives left to describe it and no one believes the re-hashed ones that are used.) (2) Is the movie violent? How much—too much for those who like their violence in small doses, or too little for those who think an evening's incomplete if there are less than a dozen corpses strewn around the place? (3) How much sex? (In case we want to take our grandchild. The child may not need to be protected against over-exposure, but Grandpa and Grandma may.) This usually requires a note at the end of the review: "Parental guidance recommended; explicit sex; frontal nudity; heavy profanity." That'll almost guarantee a lineup of teenagers halfway around the block before the doors open. And finally (4) What's the word on refreshments? Popcorn have lots of butter? A minor item, we might think, but considered vital information by our younger readers—people under fifty, that is.

Certainly, reviewing books, plays, or movies (and, of course other public exhibitions, art shows, museums, ballet, etc.) is a rewarding alternative to writing our own original books, plays, or scripts. But it should not be looked upon simply as that. It's an occupation that engages the talents of a number of highly professional writers, both full- and part-time. It allows a large measure of originality and self-expression and may serve us well in helping us to learn how to write our own compositions better.

While most of the reviewing in this country is done by nonreviewers (newspaper reporters, for instance, who are given free books and asked to review them, or authorities from different walks of life who are asked to review special interest books) we should agree that reviewing is a craft to be learned. Some of its ingredients are ours simply because we have lived so long and seen and read so much. If during our pre-retirement years we were active in literary or theatrical groups, if we lived on the fringes of the publishing or theater worlds, mingled with authors or playwrights or television producers, we'll fit naturally into the reviewing slot on the best community newspapers and magazines.

It's the same if we spent our lives strolling the halls of academe. What we need to do is look for those slots and present our credentials.

The opportunities for those of us who are seriously interested in tackling this specialized field are always likely to be limited to the smaller journals. Quite possibly, our efforts might appear alongside those of a teenager, or someone in his twenties, who is already an expert on "rock." That's O.K. Let us "elevate" the publication so that people with maturing minds may make a choice in the kind of entertainment they prefer.

What's in it for us, except free books and theater passes, the excitement of continuing to be part of the world we enjoyed, and the chance of meeting new and congenial friends? In most cases, perhaps nothing. Some of the small papers do offer an honorarium of a few bucks a column, not always at the beginning but later on if a column catches on and has provable reader appeal. (Don't ask your friends to write letters to the editor saying how much they enjoy reading your column. Editors know that particular ploy and don't like being pressured. If readers like it, editors will find out all on their own.)

When we've been on the job six months or so, we could do as the country correspondents do, organize a little syndicate of our own. We can send copies of our column to editors of other community papers in our region and tell them they can have it for five or ten dollars a week. Pick up a dozen and we might end up making as much writing informative book, theater, and movie reviews as the neighbor's teenage kid gets for mowing lawns.

But just look at the prestige, and the bookshelf full of books, and the theater and movie passes. What more should we want in our Golden Age?

Eleven

Writers in Wheelchairs

Old age is no such uncomfortable thing if one gives oneself up to it with a good grace, and don't drag it about to midnight dances and the public shows.

Horace Walpole

Most Seniors, fortunately, are in reasonably good health and have no good reason for staying away from midnight dances or public shows. They often revel in them.

They are also often able, in this new age, to dress fashionably, dine extravagantly and undertake, if it pleases them, new careers—including that of becoming writers. All without being scolded by their Juniors—or being under the necessity to pay any attention if they are.

For some, however, growing old is accompanied by physical problems that, if they are allowed, may seriously interfere with plans for a creative future. Some of us are just physically worn out—"tuckered out," as they used to say. Others may have actual physical handicaps. What kind of a future does writing offer to them?

Well, today, a lot of brave people of all ages are proving that a handicap is only as great as one allows it to be. They play championship basketball from wheelchairs, speed one-legged (or without legs) down ski slopes, hold their own international Olympics, perform on stage, and are active in all the professions and in many businesses and trades. Some of them are poets or novelists, historians or newspaper columnists.

Writing has never been a closed door for the handicapped. "Poetry is what Milton saw when he went blind," wrote the American pop poet, Donald Marquis. Elizabeth Barrett Browning was an invalid when she composed her volumes of romantic verse. And then, just to bring things up to date, let's consider the case of Helen Santmyer of Xenia, Ohio, who became famous in 1983 when she completed a 1,344 page novel from her bed in a nursing home and saw it become a Book-of-the-Month-Club selection with an initial run of 50,000 copies and the subject of a television mini-series.

Helen Santmyer was what most people would consider handicapped when she wrote "finis" to her novel about small-town Ohio life as she remembered it. She was partially blinded by cataracts and weakened by emphysema. Her book had been fifty years in the writing. As dean of the English Department at Cedarville College and later reference librarian in Dayton, Ohio, she was one of those people who knew they had a story to tell but never had the time to tell it. She did find time for two other "minor" novels, but never enough for . . . *And Ladies of the Club*, the one story she wanted most to tell. It just kept accumulating, bit by bit, page by page, till it filled eleven boxes of bookkeeper's ledger paper covered with longhand. She had reasons enough to give up when she entered the nursing home and prepared to die in peace, but no physical handicap was to be allowed to prevent her from finishing her masterpiece.

Now, her only problem is what to do with the money.

Just after Christmas, I received a letter from my new friend by correspondence, Myrtle Brodsky. She enclosed a clipping of a half-page weekend newspaper feature she had written about Christmas. Myrtle, you will remember, is in her nineties and always apologizes for her poor handwriting because she cannot see what she writes. "My intention in writing the Christmas article," she wrote, "was to make it very clear that *ninos* [her term for people over 90] need not indulge in self-pity nor require sympathy on Christmas Day. On December 5, I was alone and couldn't type, couldn't see my own handwriting, far less check, alter and polish.

"I've always found editors to be understanding people. In this case my shocking writing was accurately deciphered and the piece printed word for word. Although I cannot now see to read, I can always rely on someone reading aloud to me. Many other *ninos* are unable to get out and around in the rough winter weather and that makes reading even more important. I'm one of the lucky ones who can enjoy walking when snow and ice are the order of the day." As long as she keeps walking, Myrtle Brodsky will keep writing, finding new things to write about and a way to write them.

Finally, another old friend sent me a greeting card. In a short, handwritten sentence, he too apologized, this time for addressing the envelope on a typewriter. "My arthritis is so bad," he wrote, "I have to use two hands to write my name." This has not kept him from keeping up his regular writing schedule—a flow of correspondence with friends throughout the year.

MAKING WAY FOR THE HANDICAPPED

There are many things that most of us do without even thinking about them that are difficult for handicapped people, whether young, middle-aged, or old. But happily, we are becoming more understanding of their problems and more willing to recognize their rightful and valuable roles in society. In most communities across the country city fathers have put ramps at street crossings and entrances to public buildings; stores, hotels, and apartment buildings and most theaters and concert halls are similarly equipped, and special parking places are provided for handicapped drivers. Cars come with special devices enabling the handicapped to operate them and more importantly, perhaps, professional, industrial, and social organizations, and some government agencies have recognized the contributions handicapped people make and have taken special steps to assist them. Government grants, for instance, made it possible for a group of artists with no arms or hands to paint pictures for greeting cards and individual sale by manipulating brushes with their mouths. Instruction classes for various crafts and trades are now commonplace, and educational facilities once available only to the young and healthy are now open to the elderly and the handicapped. Even the washrooms in schools, restaurants, and other buildings now have special stalls bearing the familiar blue and white wheelchair symbol.

Like everyone who wants to write, whatever their age and physical condition, those who are handicapped must make the physical and mental efforts demanded by this most exacting profession. There are tools available for their special use if they learn how to use them, and there are literary virtues they may possess in more abundance than others because of their afflictions. They surely have greater understanding of pain and suffering, a wider appreciation of the humiliations of rejection by a society that frequently refuses to employ or even recognize them. They can write from the heart as well as the mind about the struggle to survive and triumph.

If you are a handicapped writer, you know better than anyone else what your capabilities are, but here are a few tips that may make writing a little easier.

Tape recorders make it possible for the writer who has lost the use of his hands to dictate a manuscript. And the recorder itself is no longer the heavy and cumbersome thing it used to be. Excellent voice reproduction is secured on small pocket recorders, either for making notes in a "talking" journal or writing stories or articles. Electronic typewriters with their light-touch keyboards and word processors are much easier to operate than old-style machines.

New and not yet commercially available is an exciting space-age device that will enable victims of cerebral palsy and severe, extensive paralysis to type with their eyes. Developed by two Canadian research engineers, high tech eyeglasses contain a sensor which registers the slightest eye movement and relays it to a microcomputer and printer. First models have been successfully tested with a sixteen-year-old Ottawa girl, Chantal Bedard, who cannot talk, hold a pencil, or push a computer key but has all the eye movements necessary to make the glasses work. A typing speed of twenty words a minute is an immediate possibility, opening an entirely new world to legions of those whose handicaps would otherwise prevent them from operating any kind of keyboard.

For those for whom any mechanical operations are extremely difficult if not impossible, help may often be solicited from sympathetic relatives or neighbors who may be able to take dictation and do your typing for you. Or, if these skills are lacking in your neighborhood, there are some social agencies that will arrange to have either volunteer or part-time professional typists work with you either free or for minimal charge. Do investigate the possibilities for either reading or writing help before you give up on the idea of sharing your thoughts and plots and unique experiences with others.

The deaf, to whom writing may be less of a problem but who are cut off from sounds of the world around them, are no longer denied the full benefits of television as more and more programs, particularly documentaries, are close-captioned. Devices making these captions visible to viewers are available from the telephone company and some cable television firms. Even hearing aids have improved. They are more comfortable to wear and more efficiently separate background noise from voices. Sitting in a corner with a trumpet to one's ear is now a picture of the elderly reserved for old cartoons.

Most dramatic of all aids designed for a handicapped writer is that available to the blind. I am sure that not all sightless persons are aware of how extensive that aid is. I first learned of one aspect of it when I talked to Sidney Singman, a wartime pilot who lost his sight in an air crash and now lives in France and spends his time writing books. He writes mainly nonfiction, some of it quite technical, and has published one novel. All of his work requires extensive research. I asked him how he could research a subject if he couldn't read. His answer was short: "Talking books."

Like most people, I knew a little about "talking books." There's a rack of them in the public library and I've seen them advertised, but I had no idea of the great storehouse of knowledge available free of charge to blind persons.

The Library of Congress's National Library Service Division for the Blind and Physically Handicapped, which is federally funded, provides talking books and braille books to U.S. citizens at home and abroad through state and regional libraries or direct from its Washington headquarters. Talking books are recorded in a special format of 15/16 i.p.s. on four-track cassettes, and a special playback machine, provided free, is required.

For writers like Singman, Recording for the Blind Incorporated, 20 Reszel Road, Princeton, NJ, 08540, has a collection of more than 50,000 titles available on request to individuals who are certified as being visually or physically unable to read normal printed material. A national nonprofit voluntary organization, it provides educational books on loan to individuals. All books in the collection have received copyright permission from the owners for use restricted to visually and/or physically impaired persons.

In Canada, the Canadian National Institute for the Blind, 1929 Bayview Avenue, Toronto, Ontario, M4G 3E8, is a private charitable organization offering free talking books and braille library service to Canadian citizens at home or abroad who are registered with the Institute. Through international interlibrary loans, individuals living abroad may borrow Canadian books using their local library facilities.

Singman not only makes profitable use of the free "talking books" service, he delights in it. "Once you start using 'talking books,' " he said, "you'll never want to go back to reading. Last thing at night, I go to bed, put on the earphones, relax and turn on the tape. Stories, read by professionals, come alive as they never can from a printed page. I feel that I'm privileged."

OUR WRITING SETS US FREE

Writing has never been easy, even for the able-bodied. Furthermore, it is very demanding. It got me and thousands like me out of playing bridge, becoming golf nuts, bird watching, or just plain being social. It doesn't take well to too much outside competition, which is why it wouldn't work when we were too busy to finish the stories we had to tell. Writing won't get people who can't walk out of their wheelchairs, or chronic invalids out of their bed-chambers. But it'll do something more important. It'll get them out of themselves—give them something else to think, plan, and, yes, dream about. It's better to stay awake all night worrying about how a plot for a short story is going to work out or what to write about for next week's column in the local *Gazette* than it is to toss and turn and fret about a new pain that suddenly developed in our left heel just as we were about to go to sleep.

Writing makes use of that part of our bodies that still functions as it should, our brains. Or, if it doesn't work at 100 percent capacity a session at the typewriter may help it get started again. Certainly, it'll cause confusion and emergencies and upsets and all sorts of troubles. But what's life without troubles? And handicapped people are just as entitled to have them as anybody else. Writing will, of course, have its little triumphs, too. As any good psychiatrist will tell us, concentrating one's thinking upon one problem (in this case, writing) often reduces the pressure of another (in this case, our physical handicap). It's a relief sometimes having something else that is important to remember or worry about, like, "How do I get Thorndike out of that rowboat in Cornwall before the bomb goes off?" instead of "When do I take my next pill, and is it the green one or the white one with the pink dots?"

Writing, in short, is tough, tiring, frustrating, fascinating, amusing, demanding—and damn good therapy for anyone who needs to redirect his or her thinking positively. Take it from "Dr. Knott," the self-appointed psychiatrist to would-be writers.

The worst and most common after-retirement affliction is boredom. If it's bad for people with all their physical faculties more or less intact, how much worse is it for those who are confined to an upstairs bedroom, are unable to walk, or to see, or to hear, or cannot use their hands to write or type or even feed themselves? For them, the agony of boredom is multiplied ten times. And accompanying it is a frustrating inability to express themselves or do anything about it.

Fred, a rugged, old-time Cape Codder who had been in robust health until his seventy-eighth birthday, spent his days gardening, walking, taking the odd fishing trip off the coast and driving his car to Boston for a day's shopping or a look-in at the hotel where he once worked. His evenings were devoted to lively conversations or playing bridge. Then, one morning, he woke up paralyzed, victim of a stroke. He was rushed to the hospital, given every possible treatment, then sent home—a truly handicapped person unable to wait on himself, dress, eat, or go to the bathroom unassisted. A few weeks later, he was in a nursing home. There, day after day, he sat alone in a private room, looking out the window or watching television. Sometimes he would struggle to turn the pages of a book.

When friends came to visit him his face would light up for an instant and he would try to speak to them—uttering a few angry grunts and groans as his tongue refused to obey his brain. He began to wish his visitors would stay away. He seemed destined to live out the few remaining years of his life in desperate isolation.

One day a visitor came up with a bright suggestion. Fred could still use his hands to turn the television on and off; he could turn the pages of a book: with difficulty, it was true, but he could turn them nevertheless. But he couldn't communicate, the one thing that seemed of any real importance to him.

Why not get him a small, portable typewriter, one that would fit on a shelf or tray across the arms of his chair, and let him type out his messages? He'd never used a typewriter before, but that didn't matter. His brain was still functioning. He could think. He had ideas and emotions and things he wanted to say. Slowly but surely, if he tried, he could roll in a sheet of paper, find the right keys, and with one finger, perhaps, tap by tap, put words and sentences together. Miracle of miracles—he could finally communicate. When a visitor called, he could "talk." And when he was alone, he was no longer isolated. He could write a letter to a loved one—not a long letter, but a letter just the same. Something someone else could read.

From communicating with one person it would be but a short step to communicating with many—perhaps, eventually, with the world. For Fred, left alone, memories took the place of conversation and, like Milton, the blind poet:

> A thousand fantasies
> Begin to throng into my memory,
> Of calling shapes, and beck'ning shadows dire,
> And airy tongues that syllable men's names
> On sands and shores and desert wildernesses.

Fred was discovering what writing was all about. His limbs, his muscles, and his tongue were tied; his imagination and his creative urge were free.

For those who are mobile—even if their mobility depends upon a motorized wheelchair or a specialized gearshift, or even a walker, writing may also help them get out of the house, by giving them something outside the house to do. Somewhere to go to get information—to borrow a book, to see a movie. It may also give them what they had before and never properly prized—a purpose in life, a goal to reach. And here's a nice little bonus: It could also help them earn a little money on the side.

ON AN EQUAL FOOTING

Handicapped people have almost as many choices in their writing careers as do those who are 100 percent physically fit. They don't have to be able to run the hundred-yard dash, or leap a half dozen hurdlcs in order to write a book. Nobody says they can't review a play or a movie or the latest science fiction unless they can shoot under a hundred in golf or wind-surf all Sunday afternoon.

They can attend writing courses. Almost all colleges and universities welcome and provide special facilities for handicapped students. They can certainly subscribe to correspondence courses and read books, printed ones if they can see, talking books if they can't. They can learn how to use television for more than just killing time (something that any older person should be leery of anyway since time is our most precious possession) using closed captions if they're hard of hearing. And they, perhaps better than the rest of us, can use that God-given gift supplied free of charge to almost all human beings: their imaginations.

In some cases, the handicapped may even possess advantages denied to their wholebodied neighbors who may also be striving to become writers. They can concentrate better, because they are less likely to be distracted by other interests, and they may be better writers because they know at firsthand not only the joys of living but also the pain. Alan Porter, before his death in 1942, put it this way:

> *Every Countenance*
> *That warms and lights the heart of the beholder*
> *Shews, clear and true, the signature of pain.*

People who live with disability and suffer it not always bravely but patiently may sometimes dig deeper and more honestly into their emotions, tossing aside the inhibitions that prevent their healthier fellows from giving full expression to their thoughts and feelings. Superlatives come more easily from the pens of those who have pain and suffering and frustration as their daily companions. They know the hurts of a confined life and remember, or pray for, the joys of a free one.

No one would wish to become a handicapped person simply in order to become a good writer. But for those who are afflicted, or upon whom advancing age seems to threaten new barriers to their style of living, even starting a career as an over-fifty writer does offer worthwhile compensations. Out in a world that seems to be closing itself off from them, there is a special writers' market, an editorial sanctum where the words they write will have special appeal. This market is not made up exclusively of the old. As old age becomes more popular—in the sense that more people aspire to it or at least are more likely to achieve it whether they aspire to it or not—there is a natural and very human demand for words of encouragement and a curiosity about what lies ahead.

There is a recurring demand for the ultimate in how-to books and articles—those which will supply the answer to "How Does One Cope?" Medical doctors can tell us; psychiatrists can tell us. Books by old and tiring authors of a past generation may pretend to tell us. But what those who are following want is word right from the horse's mouth—from somebody who is in there coping, seven days a week, fifty-two weeks a year, in good health or bad. They want it straight.

What does a man do when he can't hold a razor steady in the morning and almost cuts his throat every time he tries to shave? Not a momentous, world-shaking question, perhaps, but mighty important to a fifty-year-old who thinks he detects the first signs of palsy. What does a retired woman, crippled with arthritis, do when her husband asks her to sew a button on his coat—something she quit doing before she went to law school and took up again when she retired as a judge? Nothing there to stir the militant minds of women's libbers but of some concern to some about-to-be-retired woman who has arthritic symptoms. And how does Myrtle Brodsky travel about the countryside in all kinds of weather when she can't even see enough to read her own handwriting? That's one question to which there is an answer. Myrtle turns out how-to-cope articles every month and gets them published.

There are more generalized questions, too, questions that are being asked by younger handicapped people who have been cared for by relatives or friends and are now in danger of being left to manage on their own. How does one go about choosing a retirement residence or nursing home and what's there to do once one gets there? And, "Any suggestions for a new career? I don't want to just vegetate but they can't keep me on where I am any longer." What they all want is the Voice of Experience—not theories, not programs: just "I was there and this is how it is."

A BOOK IN EACH OF US

For every handicapped person, there's a book to be written. It may be humorous or tragic, straight facts or damn right angry. It could be a short story, a magazine article, or a handicapped's eye view of a movie, a book, or a television show that tries to help the uninitiated find their way around in what is a strange new world. Written by someone who has conquered a disability or learned how to live with one, it can be a message of hope and encouragement to others to do likewise.

Twentieth-century America is the product of the success story. It began with Horatio Alger's *Tom the Bootblack* and other classics of the work-hard, be-honest, count-your-pennies (marry the boss's daughter) genre. Then came the magazines, like the original, *American*, a monthly journal publishing a collection of stories of successful Americans; then *Saturday Evening Post*, which mixed fact and fiction to publicize the American dream, and eventually *Fortune*, dedicated to telling the story of the millionaires and the five hundred top American companies. Styles and trends change but the message is still there today, loud and clear. Why else would *Search for Excellence* be on the top of the 1983 best-seller lists and "How to Make Money" seminars be the stars of the international hotel banquet room and convention hall circuit?

Today, men and women, successful and not so successful, are peering into their futures, not at sixty or sixty-five but when they're just well into middle age. They know they are going to live longer. The statistics say so. They know, some of them, they're going to have physical problems, as well as financial ones. They're preparing for the latter now: investing money in tax-deferred retirement funds, checking out retirement villages or smaller houses or condominiums, reading medical books. They're also becoming curious about how they're going to cope when the "office" is no longer there to support them, their spouse is dead or divorced or just disappeared, the kids are as mixed up as they were—single-parenting, married and divorced, moved to another city or another country and about to be all on their own. They're looking for a new kind of success story—*How to Succeed After 60 Without Even Trying* would suit them just fine.

Those of us who have learned how to cope the hard way, and also learned how to tell others how to do the same, have a potential market waiting. Enough to keep us out of the house, away from boredom, and back in the "real" world for some years to come.

Answers to the questions "Who publishes that kind of after-fifty literature?" and "What does one do to reach them?" are to be found in the next chapter. Meanwhile, it's time to sit down and do some serious thinking. If we're handicapped, how well are we coping? Is this something other similarly handicapped people can do? If so, how can we help them and when do we get started?

Seems like "right now" might be the answer.

TWELVE

Anyone Out There Listening?

Do you know, considering the market there are more
Poems produced than any other thing!
No wonder poets sometimes have to seem
So much more business-like than businessmen.
Their wares are so much harder to get rid of.

Robert Frost, *New Hampshire*

It's work, the reading, and researching, hustling about the countryside, writing and rewriting and correcting and checking the spelling and the punctuation and the language. It's fun, too. And it's all part of being a writer.

But eventually, we come to the bottom line. What's the going price per word? And how we go about getting it?

What does one do with all the words and the sentences and the pages of manuscripts after one has been to school, gathered expert opinions, talked to teachers and cousins and aunts and uncles and prepared everything according to professional instructions—name and address in the upper left-hand corner, double-spaced and wide margins and a self-addressed stamped envelope enclosed?

Is there really someone out there listening—checkbook in hand, and pen hovering—ready to put down some solid, hard-earned cash for what we in our late years have just learned how to produce? And finally, is it really true that there's a real, no-foolin', cash-paying market especially for old-timers like us who are just bustin' into the racket?

Yes, Virginia, there is. All we've got to do is have faith and do a lot of looking and plugging and we'll find it.

Bob Lane, the free-lance writer who awhile back told us something about word processors, sold about fifty magazine articles in the first two years after he retired in the fall of 1981. Fees ranged from $15 for a two hundred word book review to $1,400 for a thirty-five hundred word article with two sidebars. Working approximately half-time, he made more than $10,000 from writing in

1983. And this is what he says about the market for older writers: "There is no age discrimination associated with selling one's words, which will stand or fall strictly on their own merit." And to all of us looking for subjects, he says: "The subjects I write are mostly drawn from my past incarnations. 'The Louse' was about playing marbles in French Lick, Indiana, prior to World War II. 'The Art of the Take-Over' was an interview with Frank Carlucci, deputy secretary of defense, with whom I once worked."

Getting started is the big problem. Should we send our precious manuscript to an editor unbidden? What editor? We look in *Writer's Market* and in the monthly issues of *Writer's Digest* or *The Writer* and there are hundreds of editors listed. Isn't it a bit like buying a lottery ticket and hoping we get a winner at odds of a thousand to one? Perhaps we should appoint an agent instead and let him or her go looking for the editor for us. But someone told us agents don't like one-time authors, and aren't they just going to say, "You're too old—no future for me in taking on someone who's already in retirement. No thanks, Grandma (or Grandpa), better do your own thing"?

Well, let's be honest and put all our cards on the table. We've spent some time, sweat, and blood (and probably some money) learning how to write. The result of all that expenditure is sitting in front of us now, almost screaming for us to do something about it. We've got to stop being just writers for a while and start thinking about learning how to sell. Some good solid market research is in order.

"AVON CALLING . . ."

It's a funny thing about writers, young as well as old. They sweat and they swear and they toil and they struggle to write something that's good enough to read. They'll go through hell and high water to find the right word and compose the proper phrase, stay up all night, fight with the neighbors, and yell at the typewriter. But tell them they've got to go to work to sell what they've written and they'll hold up their hands in horror. They didn't get into the writing business just to end up as salesmen. If they'd wanted to become peddlers they might just as well have signed up with Avon and gone door-to-door pounding. They'd have met more people that way, and maybe made more money as well.

They forget, or maybe they never knew, that most artists who got into painting pictures didn't figure they'd end up peddling paintings either. But they lug their canvases from gallery to gallery, or fill their studios with cocktail-drinking "patrons" at exhibit openings or they wheedle a review out of a local art critic— all to help sell their daubs. Many of the best of them wrapped their masterpieces in newspapers and swapped them for a meal and a glass of wine at a café, and sometimes were overpaid.

When I was in business, we sometimes needed an extra hand and would advertise for someone who could write to come to work in our public relations department. In they'd troop, youngsters, oldsters, middle-aged men and women, all eager to be P.R. types like on television. Their first comments, after introducing themselves as applicants: "I hope there's no selling involved." And the second: "Do you have a pension plan?" They would never get it into their little heads that if they got the job and if every time they visited a client they didn't do a selling job there soon wouldn't be any salaries, let alone money for pensions.

We might as well make up our minds that in free-lancing, writing is just half the job (unless we do it for pleasure). Selling is the other half. And one more word before we end this lugubrious note on the ultimate fate of all successful writers: There are more writers than editors, more manuscripts than publishers and millions more written words than column inches available to print them in. We who write live in a buyer's market and as Geoffrey Chaucer, one of the early members of our tribe, reported in his prologue to the *Wife of Bath's Tale* (as paraphrased by Alexander Pope, another one of our gang), "A glutted market makes provision cheap."

There goes our dream of a fortune overnight. But with that limitation, we still have quite a few choices in what is always an active market. We should rejoice in the fact that in this topsy-turvy world we are one of the few surviving species engaging in free and open competition. There are no writer conglomerates.

Here goes. We put on our selling shoes and:

  1. We take what we've written, pick a name out of a publishers' directory and send it out with a hope and a prayer that it'll sell itself. If it does, we're one in a million. We've hit the jackpot

first time around. We should try our luck at Monte Carlo or Las Vegas; we'd probably break the bank. If, as is more likely, the manuscript comes tumbling back, we can mail it again and again and repeat the process until it is covered with inky fingerprints and we become so worn out we give up and go back to playing solitaire.

2. We can be very scientific and very selective, study the market, read the magazines or books published by our chosen quarries, make the changes that seem necessary to meet their indicated requirements and go back to the post office. This has a little better chance than Number 1.

3. We can take a marketing course and learn what sells a product and then apply that knowledge to the piece of merchandise we're putting up for grabs. For that's what it is, folks, a cardboard box or an envelope full of the product of our minds and writing skills which we fervently hope will interest a rich and generous buyer. Unlike most other producers of goods for sale, though, we depend entirely upon the buyer to set the price if he or she chooses to buy.

In the learning process we'll be told that the product must be right, not just for us and the professor who's teaching us but for the editor who's going to be asked to look at it and (here's a real stopper) for the marketing manager of the publishing house that's going to print it. He or she will probably have the final say, because no matter how much the editor may love us and all our works, the person responsible for selling copies and helping the publisher stay alive and pay royalties is going to make the ultimate decision.

THE RULES OF THE GAME

But we've got to get past the editor first, so let's imagine what he or she wants in addition to a nice, clean-typed manuscript and an interesting story. Sensible editors like to know who we are, what else we have written, if anything, what our book or article is all about, and whether or not we are authorities or especially knowledgeable about the subject. They also dislike having to wade through a long, involved manuscript and would prefer that we send a "salesman's sample": a synopsis, table of contents, and perhaps a one-page letter describing the reader market as we see it. If it's a magazine article we're selling, a query first is preferred. A query saves time and money and will probably be read, which is something unsolicited articles sometimes are not.

If we're going to be businesslike and try to make a little money out of all our efforts, then we'd better get a firm grasp on the basics. To appreciate all the gory details spelled out by experts we should consult the section headed "The Business of Freelancing" at the back of *Writer's Market.* Meanwhile, it'll help if we learn:

1. To conform to editors' preferences for manuscripts that are cleanly typed, double-spaced with one-inch left margins, on plain white, 8½x11 sheets of good 25 percent cotton fiber paper;

2. To mail our submissions to book publishers as unbound, loose sheets in ream-size stationery boxes; to magazine editors, in 10x12 envelopes. In both cases, SASE (self-addressed stamped envelopes), should be enclosed. International stamp coupons for out of country mailings can be purchased at the post office.

3. To write and use effective queries to editors. These constitute our sales pitch and in the long run may be as important as our manuscripts. An editor will respond to a good query that tells him who we are, what it is we are writing about, who we are writing it for, and how long it is. For book editors, we'd be wise to include a short synopsis, table of contents, and one or two sample chapters. If our subject is nostalgic, something about all our yesterdays, mentioning our advanced age could be a help. (Otherwise, keep it a secret.) The response may not be the one we're looking for but at least we'll have a rejection slip to show the income tax auditor if he questions our deduction for postage expenses.

Having gone to all this trouble to get a foot in the door, as it were, we must now be ready to comply with the sometimes ridiculous demands of editors we have solicited with all good will. We will be told to cut the manuscript in half, increase it by eleven hundred words, reverse the order of chapters, eliminate the most colorful descriptive passages, add some more exciting location identifications, move the plot from Inner Mongolia to lower Basin Street, put some sex in, take some sex out (not very likely).

Not all editors are eccentrics, but it's reasonable to assume that those who react positively to our sales pitch probably will be. One of them, one day, may frighten us into writing a best seller for,

> *It's not learning, grace nor gear*
> *Nor easy meat and drink,*
> *But bitter pinch of pain and* fear
> *That makes creation think.*

So said Rudyard Kipling, obviously in response to some editor's cruel prodding.

CORNERING THE MARKET

Our marketing education complete, we are now ready to look at that special section of the market which seems to be most suitable for after-fifty writers. It won't be ours alone; some brash young brats will try to muscle in on it, but we'll have the advantage because of our experience, the fact that we are "on track" and not merely guessing, and because we supposedly have greater knowledge and the time to work on it.

Here are some of the markets we should look at:

1. *If we choose to take the journalist route,* as newspaper correspondents, book, theater, or movie reviewers, or sports reporters:

(a) The local newspaper, community weekly, or city magazine, not overlooking the give-away sheets that pay peanuts but get us in print. Personal contact with editors, taking along samples, is the best approach.

(b) Larger regional, or even metropolitan newspapers that may be looking for local correspondents. Again, personal contact with editors, toting a bag of samples and an outline of our qualifications (we've lived there a long time, know everybody, worked with the waterworks department, etc.) is recommended.

(c) If we become regular columnists like book reviewers, legal advisers, etc., we could try for multiple sales by sending copies of our printed columns to nearby publications or by writing, enclosing samples, to one of the syndicates. (A list of syndicate editors is published each July in a special issue of *Editor and Publisher.*) If we get an acceptance there, we could be in for some real money.

Jud Arnold, a former Monsanto marketing executive, retired to devote full-time to his principal hobby, gardening. He wrote a few short horticultural articles, submitted them to the editor of the local newspaper, and became its weekly garden columnist. After a few months, his column was sold to a syndicate which in turn sold it to newspapers across the country. Later the column, together with some new material, became part of an encyclopedia of gardening. Promoting the encyclopedia led to radio and television interviews and finally a contract for a weekly spot on television. What's next? Maybe a network program and then, perhaps, a movie or a musical with the former marketing expert *cum* writer strolling down the garden path.

2. *If we have a bit of a "name" or a reputation* in some specialized field—politics, law, medicine, the arts, technology, business, etc.:

(a) We may go for the Op-Ed pages of local journals with occasional articles and comments on our specialties. This means we must keep up-to-date and not just live in the past. We must use our past experience to explain current events. If we can make ourselves known to editors, either by personal contacts or by addresses to local clubs and associations and establish ourselves as authorities, a sale will be easier.

(b) Periodicals that serve our professions or businesses could be interested in articles, either occasionally or on a weekly or monthly basis, that offer their readers the "Voice of Experience" and are helpful to those on the way up.

(c) The weekend supplements of metropolitan dailies (there are more than 150 of them in the U.S.) buy articles from knowledgeable freelancers. Lists of editors and their special interests are published in writer's magazines and directories.

(d) The periodicals of opinion we like to read either because we share their opinions or hate them. These, the so-called "Quality Group," go for the kind of quiet, thoughtful articles we who have lots of time on our hands should be able to write.

(e) A venture away from the printed word and into the world of sound might lead us to a spot on radio or television, if we provide well-written scripts and can present them with verbal skill.

3. *If nostalgia is our thing* (Here's the bonanza market and we're here at just the right time.):

(a) Many newspapers and magazines (including some of the best) are in the market for reminiscences or flashbacks. We are living in a period that is going to be increasingly obsessed with what happened fifty, seventy-five, and a hundred years ago, because we are approaching century's end. There will be a great rash of articles about our world as it used to be when the century was young and we were, too. We have the edge because it's us we'll be writing about. Colorful, accurate writing about even the humblest subjects, with good old-time illustrations, will be in big demand, so let's get down the old snapshot albums and start going through the files.

(b) What applies to the general newspaper and periodical field goes double for the specialized publications. Scientific journals will be hungry for articles by one-time scientists about their early days in the lab; a barber with a good memory for names and some interesting former clients might manage a series of barber-chair interviews. Business publications will want company histories, old-time stories about days in primitive factories and offices. Again, old photographs or drawings may help sell the story.

(c) Perhaps an industry, a company, a church, or association in our community will also be having a 100th birthday when the century ends and will want to capitalize on their record. There'll be a booming market for writers of commemorative books or booklets. We have more time to research these stories, and have our own memories to buttress our facts. We've lived almost as long as they have, so why not have them publish their old-time records written by old-time writers? "Centenarian Writes Company's Centenary History" makes a nice headline. We should also know that nonpublishing companies often pay better than those in the business.

4. *If fiction is our forte:*
(a) Any magazine, weekend supplement, or newspaper that uses fiction is a prospect for us, but here, except for the unusual circumstances caused by century's end, we are in direct competition with younger writers. The nostalgia bit is our biggest plus. Some editors are already beginning to look for some good-old-days romances and there'll be lots of television and radio programmers looking for writing pioneers.

(b) Book publishers: Books of reminiscences, old photographs, tales of the pioneers will be everywhere—from table tops to paperbacks. We'll be in the money if we're old railway buffs, or onetime suffragettes, and if we've learned to write. The big problem will be a glut of manuscripts. Everybody and his or her dog will be trying to get in on the act, so it's time we got moving now. We shouldn't overlook the stories we were too young to be involved in but heard from our parents and our grandparents. There'll be tremendous interest in stories of World War I, the Great Depression, fashions as they were and how they changed, the foods we ate and didn't eat in the twenties, the songs we sang and the movie stars we idolized. Nobody will expect us to be very articulate about the Indian Wars or conquering of the West, but old journals and diaries, plus remembered conversations with those who were old when we were young may provide all the research aids we need. In any case, we should be jogging our memories, getting them into shape, warming up the typewriter, and preparing for a book—perhaps just a local one (try a small publisher) or a more ambitious one that could interest a major publisher looking for a full-length autobiography or a novel.

5. *If we're poets at heart:*
If it's money we're after, we've picked a tough territory to mine. As poet Robert Frost remarked, we've got to be pretty smart business people if we hope to sell our poetry. Still, there are some market possibilities.

(a) Many poetry magazines not only accept but solicit poems from far and near. I had a letter from one of them just recently, urging me to enter a poem in a prize contest, and I'm not even a poet. The pay is poor, sometimes consisting of a couple of copies of the issue in which our work appears, but a lot of poets get published and sometimes one of them is "discovered." Some newspapers and magazines also publish short poems (as fillers, I'm afraid) but pay little for them and may even charge for publishing them.

(b) If we're really quite good, there are book publishers willing to take a chance on books of poetry even though they'll probably lose money on them. When we're in a bookshop next time we should take a look at the shelves marked "Poetry" or "Literature." There will be a surprisingly large number of titles there, many of them recent releases. If we find one that appeals to us and contains the kind of poems we like to write, then we can hustle back home and put a batch in the mail to that publisher.

(c) There are some anthologies printed in which we might be included. Usually prior publication in some reputable journal is required.

That about completes the "commercial" outlets list. The choice is wide, but before we begin submitting queries or synopses, we'd better study very carefully the publications or publishers we select. Only when we are very well aware of the type of material they buy and publish should we offer them our products, and then we should make sure it conforms in every possible way to their general pattern. Off-beat pieces sometimes get by, but our chances are better when we follow an acceptable formula. Believe me, in this manuscript-selling business, the customer (editor, marketing manager, publisher) is always right—even when he or she is wrong.

There is one more option we have before we get off the money kick and onto writing just for fun. We can go semicommercial and be our own publisher. A risky business, you'll say, but a poet, of all people, who lives in the Finger Lakes district of upstate New York has proved that one can make a decent little income out of writing and selling poetry. Ralph Seager is now into his seventies. After producing several commercially published volumes of poetry, he decided to cut out the middle-man. He published at his own expense a volume of regionally oriented and seasonal verse, and persuaded several bookstores and gift shops within about a sixty-mile radius to stock it. From this enterprise, he makes as much or more than we would likely do from peddling little filler items to suburban newspapers.

The man I mentioned away back who wrote a book about fox hunting in Ireland and couldn't find a publisher went ahead on his own and produced a handsome illustrated volume that he sells for forty-five dollars a copy. I met him on the street a few weeks after Christmas. He'd sold two thousand out of the three thousand copies he'd printed and was preparing for a second edition. "If I sell five thousand altogether, I'll make a pretty profit," he said, "and if I sell ten thousand, I'll be rich." He'd just received letters or calls from three publishers who had previously turned him down.

And that brings us to:

6. *Writers for the joy of it:*

Fortunately, opportunities for seeing our writing in print do not end with commercial publishers. Many of us are in no great need of money, have no great ambition to head the best-seller list and would be quite content if we could share our ideas, fantasies, and love of writing with a few sympathetic readers. For us there are any number of specialized publications, vanity presses, and small printers willing to help us self-publish. There are, in fact, far more editors waiting for after-fifty contributions than could be listed in a single volume. Many of them we have to hunt and dig out for ourselves.

(a) For fun primarily—though a little money wouldn't hurt: Try magazines, newspapers, and newsletters published by organiza tions like the American Association of Retired Persons (*Modern Maturity*, a slick, professionally produced monthly, pays for good articles; the *AARP Newsletter*, a monthly, uses articles without pay); Action for Independent Maturity (*Dynamic Years*, a monthly devoted to providing those over fifty with good how-tos for retirement, pays very well) and the Gray Panthers. (Their *Bulletin*, a monthly tabloid newspaper, likes hard-hitting items but does not pay.) Note: Age alone won't guarantee an acceptance of our efforts by these Senior magazines. To win a place in these editors' publications, we must be as professional as they are.

(b) For fun and self-satisfaction only: In Canada and the United States there are some 50,000 branches of Senior Citizen associations and many more independent groups organized in YMCA's, leisure clubs, and community centers. Many of these publish weekly or monthly newspapers or newsletters, sometimes typewritten and duplicated, sometimes printed offset by volunteer members, and sometimes produced in small local print shops. Editors of these publications have one common problem. They are short of the kind of editorial material that makes a publication worth publishing. Constantly appealing to members for contributions of essays, memoirs, poems, how-tos and the like, they are swamped by responses. Unhappily, most of the stuff they publish is bad—poorly written, often ungrammatical or factually inaccurate, and almost never properly edited. The result is a tremendous amount of drivel foisted upon readers who deserve better. Anything we can do to improve the level of writing in these thousand of little publications should earn us a place in some literary Valhalla even if it doesn't produce a capitalist penny.

(c) For a good cause: Churches, clubs, associations, and societies that publish "house" magazines and newspapers or quarterly and annual reports are in a similar predicament. They have countless volunteer contributors who can't write, and they're ignored by those of us who don't see them as a "market," albeit a free one, for our output. They, too, need semiprofessional help—contributions from writers who have learned how to spell and compose proper sentences who could, at the very least, rewrite some of the submitted material. This is a volunteer exercise we could enjoy; it will help sharpen our skills and prepare us for bigger things to come. Writers who write—even for free—almost always get better.

A SHARED JOY
Writing for the joy of it is a bit of a hobby of mine, as some of you may have gathered, and since I wrote a book under that title in 1983 I've been astonished to learn how many people not only share my enthusiasm but have invented all sorts of ways to do it.

Norman Wilner of San Francisco writes, "I've been teaching creative writing for fifteen years and had thousands of students. I tell them all, 'Writing is fun, writing is therapy, writing is lucrative,' but first and foremost is the fun, 'the pure joy of it.' Writing is a labor of love. I call it 'my healthy neurosis.' I just finished a three-act play which took me six months and I enjoyed every single minute of it." (That's another potential market I overlooked for any of us who have had careers or part-time hobbies in the theater. Countless small amateur acting groups yearn for locally written plays or skits they can perform without paying royalties, and those of us who can do better can always try for the professional stage. The key word for us is *experience*. We won't need to learn how theaters work if we've spent a half century or so backstage.)

Eula (Merry) Harris is another write-for-fun enthusiast. A cancer patient in a California hospital, she writes: "I've had it both ways, as a professional photo-journalist and as a hobby writer— and there is far more pleasure in writing what one *wants* to write than in writing what is saleable. . . . There are several international organizations for amateur writers and publishers. It's a good idea to learn how to be a 'pro,' if that's one's ambition, by belonging to such an organization." Eula closes by saying if there are senior writers among us who'd like more information, they should send their name and a SASE and she'll gladly share her knowledge of amateur journalism. (Eula Merry Harris, publisher, *The Roadrunner*, P.O. Box 25, Ocotillos, CA 92259.)

If we dig hard enough, look into dusty corners and read "little magazines," personal ads in literary publications, and out-of-the-way papers, we'll find some unusual and quite fascinating ways to play the writing game. Many of us, for instance, may like to write letters but can't find the kind of stimulating correspondent we need. We look upon letter-writing as more than just a "hello-how-are-you" hasty note; we want to explore ideas, exchange opinions, maybe get involved in controversies with some other like-minded person.

Stephen Sikora, a carpenter in Albany, California, has just what we're looking for. Stephen's a letter-writing nut, too. So a few years ago he set up a Letter Writers' Network, which eventually became the Readers' League, and now publishes a *Catalogue of Correspondence* which introduces letter writers to each other. Our literary life will continue to decline, he believes, if "we amateur writers leave all our writing and thinking in the hands of a few professionals. In order to do at least some of the writing for ourselves, I can think of no better means than that of private letters."

If we have a yen to write to someone who may not share our ideas but shares an interest in them, we can send Mr. Sikora a dollar and he'll send us a copy of his catalogue. Then, if we spot an ad by a likely correspondent we write that person in care of the Reader's League, Box 6218, Albany, CA 94706. (The ad is coded, and our reply may be, too, so that neither of us knows who we are corresponding with until we have received the first letter. We may then reply using our own name and address. If we don't like what we get, we just discontinue the whole thing.)

Sikora points out that his original advertisers included people of various interests and ages (the twenties through the nineties). Some seek exchanges of letters only on specific topics with a few specific people. One Russian expatriate wishes to talk to a fellow countryman while others seek correspondence with fellow-runners, journal writers, Arabs interested in politics in the Middle East, or with parents of kids hooked on video games.

Suppose, though, that no one has an ad that interests us? Then we buy our own. An ad in the *Catalogue* costs four dollars for fifty words; two dollars for each additional ten words.

WRITERS' GAMES

Finally, for the way-out, special-special interest writer, there's the Fanzine Club in Garland, Texas, and, according to my informant, hundreds of other fanzine clubs across America. What a "fanzine" is and how it works was explained in a letter Cheree T. Cargill, of Garland, wrote to the editors of *Writer's Digest*. "As an amateur writer," she related, "I have long endured well-meaning family and friends urging me to write professionally. No amount of explanation will convince them that writing is a hobby to me and I do it for the pure enjoyment I get out of it, the same as I enjoy my needlepoint and cross-stitch.

"However, there is a little-known area of amateur writing—fan publications or fanzines. Dealing with popular television shows or movies, such as 'Star Trek' and *Star Wars*, there are over 100 fanzines currently available, all written, illustrated and published by people who do it solely for the love of it. They are strictly nonprofit publications, usually limited to less than two hundred copies per issue. While riding a fine line on copyright laws, these publications have the tacit approval of [companies like] Lucasfilm and Paramount. All parties take pains to stay in each other's good graces, the fans because they really have no formal legal consent to write their stories, the studios because these are the people who pay to see their movies, sometimes dozens of times.

"Besides the TV and movie fanzines, there are also those dealing with straight science fiction and fantasy, western fiction, satire and even the roles of specific actors such as Harrison Ford."

Anyone interested in studying—or starting—a fanzine, is invited to write Cheree Cargill at 457 Meadowhill Drive, Garland, Texas 75043 and send along a self-addressed stamped envelope (no money). They'll get a sample fanzine in return.

In these United States and Canada there must be countless other equally fun writers' games to be played. (If not, there's nothing to stop us from inventing ones of our own.) If one of us uncovers enough of them, we might have the material for a magazine article or book. A *Wacky Writers' Game Book* might find a place on the market.

We need only look at Thames and Hudson, the prestigious international art book publisher of London, for an example of how not to take writing too seriously. T & H sometimes get tired of being proper publishers and like to have some fun. In 1982, they decided to print a book a year chosen from unsolicited manuscripts received which they believed had the least likely prospects of success. In 1982, it was *Pigs in Art* and in 1983, *Two Hundred Ways to Tie Your Necktie Through the Ages.*

THIRTEEN

The Last Roundup

No Clock	*No Phone*
R E T I R E D	
No Address	*No Money*

The time has come to make up our minds. Do we really want to begin a new career or even totter on the edge, making it a part-time hobby only? Is completing that unfinished story or taking a fling at photo-journalism so all-fired important, or are we just anxious to find out if we can do it? Are the rewards sufficient to justify the sacrifices we will have to make, the disappointments we may suffer?

It's not just the money—nor the fun—nor just keeping active and out of trouble—that makes us do it. There's more to writing after fifty than that. If we have a real feel for it and manage to cope with the pressures, frustrations, and discouragements that are at some time or other every writer's lot, writing may create for us a whole new way of life. It can give us a zip and a verve we never had before and help us mentally, physically, financially, and even socially to make our second half century the most useful and rewarding years of our lives.

And that's the real bottom line.

Jack Dukes Sr., of Hastings, Minnesota, illustrates perfectly the positive values of writing one's way into retirement. He discovered what it could do for him when he took to the typewriter after a two-decade business career that had ended in broken health, bankruptcy, and divorce at age forty-seven. Three years later, helped by a Minneapolis writers' workshop, he won the National Writers' Club short story contest for his entry, "The Trapper and the Fox," and three other awards for essays, poetry and photography. Today, he is a new man, liberated by his ability to write.

Mr. Dukes's experience doesn't represent the general idea of what people should do when approaching or living in retirement. My son, age forty-nine and nearer to becoming a Senior Citizen than he likes to think, comes closer to presenting the stereotyped thinking about old age. At Christmas in 1984, a gorgeously wrapped auto license plate was his specially selected gift for his father. On it was the message that graces the opening of this chapter. I'm sure he expected me to attach it to the two-door Toyota to which I have descended while he still travels to and from his office in his multigadgeted BMW. Instead, I suspended it from the handle bars of the Exercycle which is one of my writing career accessories. Two miles on the cycle, three hours or six pages at the typewriter and voila! out comes a book.

The message was wrong, of course, on all four counts. The same 150-year-old Seth Thomas clock that kept time for my grandfather gets me up at 8:00 A.M. It chimes its way to midnight faster than ever. I have three telephones in my single-floor flat. I'm not as nimble as I once was and I avoid running up and down the hall every time Ma Bell beckons. My address, including ZIP Code, is well enough known that something drops through the letter box almost every day, taking only a couple of weeks longer to reach me than mail did thirty years ago. And, as for money, I'm rolling in it. I made almost as much last year from book royalties, lecture fees, and radio or television talks as I made as a cub reporter in the 1920s. Salary then: twelve dollars a week!

OVER FIFTY—AND PROUD OF IT!
I admit to being a Senior Citizen writer and don't find the title either demeaning or demoralizing. I'm not above using my age as a lever to spark an interest among those editors or program directors who regard anything that happened before 1970 as potentially usable folklore and are amazed to find themselves talking to anyone who can actually remember World War I.

I've had thirty years' writing experience since the age of fifty and learn something new every day. I know something about the problems "over the hill" writers face. I'm often miserably aware of anxieties caused by long waits for replies from editors or publishers and suffer through the long gestation periods between editor acceptance and final publication. Frustrations and sometimes angry outbursts are also part of the bottom line for every writer who hopes to be professional, and we must learn to live with

them. Some are like William Kennedy, of Albany, New York, who
sent his book manuscript to thirteen publishers and kept getting
it back. Then he remembered that he had once met Saul Bellow at
a writer's conference and they had corresponded occasionally. He
told him about his experiences. Bellow asked to see the manuscript, read it, liked it, and sent it to his publisher, Viking Press in
New York (one of the thirteen who had rejected it). Viking
published it. Kennedy's novel *Ironweed* won a Pulitzer Prize and
another money award for a quarter of a million dollars. And he
was suddenly in demand. After writing for thirty years without
much success, Bill Kennedy finally made it in his mid-fifties.
And that's what keeps us all dreaming, isn't it?

Believe me, a six months' wait for an editor's reply to a manuscript submission or query is a lot longer at eighty than it was at
fifty. Did I say six months? Well, how about this? When I was a
young and hearty seventy-eight, I was full of beans and thankful
that another book-length manuscript was finished and in an editor's hands. Fifteen cajoling letters and six long-distance telephone calls later, as I passed quickly from seventh to my eighth
decade, an acceptance letter finally arrived.

There I was, contract in hand. My advance royalty check was in
the bank. Four or five months of rigorous editing and rewriting
lay ahead. Six months later the book would be printed. I counted
the hours and had no difficulty reminding myself that the real
bottom line certainly wasn't money. If it were, we'd all be better
off emulating my young friend "Mr. Sandman," polishing floors
out there on the Pacific coast or hiring on as plumbers' or dress-
makers' assistants.

If it's not money, what? Other rewards may be just as evasive.
Some retired professionals, for instance, seek their compensation
by creating written memorials to their long careers and find equal
frustrations. A large metropolitan hospital made it known that it
was planning to have written a comprehensive and popular-style
history that might even attract a commercial publisher. Just retired from the staff was a chief surgeon of considerable renown
who expressed an interest in writing it and whose name on the
cover would give the volume prestige. After two years of what
was obviously difficult work on his part, the surgeon delivered a
two-hundred-page typed manuscript to the directors. It was filled

with interesting information but completely lacking in human interest or style. The board then called in a thoroughly experienced professional writer and suggested he collaborate with the doctor and produce a readable and publishable text.

The doctor, concerned primarily about "protecting" his manuscript and ensuring that it was "his" monument, did not refuse to cooperate. He was, in fact, too cooperative. At every suggestion of a correction or addition he volunteered to write the new copy, thus adding to the problem. It soon became obvious the project would never be completed. The doctor wasn't happy; the professional writer was frustrated. The board decided to accept the original manuscript, have ten or twelve mimeographed copies nicely bound and deposited in local medical libraries as the doctor's memoirs. A writer was then engaged to start a new history from scratch.

This closing chapter sums up the pros and cons of an end-of-life writing career. Should I or shouldn't I? This is the last roundup; after this, you're on your own.

Here, we take a look at our assets and liabilities, make our choices and measure our prospects, all with a view to helping us reach that Great Decision and avoid the pitfalls that could translate joy into misery. Are we ready to jump in and join the race for fame, fun, some social prestige, and possible money—or for simpler rewards? Next week or next month may be too late. Since the decision we make will be in many ways as important as the career decision we made years ago, it behooves us to give the move serious consideration and to discuss it with others who are likely to be affected by it—including a spouse, if we have one, who expects to share the pleasures as well as the sorrows of our declining years.

Nowhere in this book have I promised you roses, nor even a healthy crop of dandelions. And I must remind you once again that there are millions of others just like us on this continent who are, and will continue to be, seeking recognition in the writers' marketplace. Only a few thousand at most will scale the heights; and often, as we read their works and then examine our own, we'll wonder what got them there. Another few thousand will obtain some satisfaction as literary journeymen (or journeywomen, if there are such things), paid by the inch for their contributions or rewarded simply by seeing their names in print. The rest of us will keep on, wondering what happened to our carefully written little masterpieces or our jingles and bits of neighborhood news that never got published. What should we have done differently? Who along the way could have helped us? Who, if anyone, went out of his or her way to frustrate us? Should we, in fact, ever have attempted to do what so many others have tried and failed?

We must remember, as we assemble our assets, that in our free enterprise system, we writers are the ultimate entrepreneurs. Those who write books gather the raw materials, do the research, sometimes design and create the prototype, craft the semifinished products, find a manufacturer-buyer, make necessary repairs and refinements, participate in product testing (proofreading), check artwork and layout and sometimes prepare an index. They then often go out on the firing line and help sell the blasted thing in bookshops, on radio and television networks, in newspaper interviews, and on lecture tours. If all their efforts are successful, they may make a profit. And the government will come along and take a big chunk of it away.

Those of us who choose the less exotic writing arenas (small-town journalism, trade paper or magazine writing, for instance) are spared some of the book writer's tribulations. For one thing, we don't spend a year or two creating a product and we usually get faster rejections or acceptances. But we are all private-enterprisers just the same. Only on the surface are we all gentle participants in some kind of literary game. We who enter the writing field at fifty or later will find, as we found twenty or thirty years ago when we began our first careers, that it's a jungle out there. Our big advantage now is that we don't have to enter the jungle in order to eat.

There's one more "hazard" to contend with. Are we physically and mentally equipped to begin a new full- or part-time career, particularly in a field which many consider esoteric and which may be far removed from any previous working experience? Are we prepared to put up with the skepticism or downright derision of friends and relatives who will openly suggest we have gone off our heads and should be doing something useful, like gardening or baking pies or collecting stamps? Can we face up to meeting our oldest friend when we're out picking up the morning newspaper and hear him ask us what we're trying to prove? "Why not sit back and enjoy retirement? You worked hard all your life. You have enough to live on. You're entitled to a rest." I know half a dozen retirees for whom that's just the right prescription. For them, a life of ease, even with limited resources, is what they worked for, and they're not about to go back to slogging their way through the rest of their lives. For these, two weeks on the beach at Panama City make up for forty years of the daily grind.

If we're men contemplating a new post-retirement career, what about our wives? What about the "little woman," as we used to call her before we realized that the home manager was one of the hardest working, most talented, underpaid, and, worse, unrecognized workers in society? Isn't she entitled to get a crack at doing what she's always wanted to do, now that her husband is home and able to take on part of the housekeeping? And what if she's the one who wants a writing career?

"Spousely" support and neighborhood understanding are important environmental conditions for a writer in retirement.

Now, keeping all the above in mind and realizing that in spite of all the difficulties and disappointments there are still thousands who succeed, many of them "after-fifty" beginners, why not give it a go? Who knows, we may discover that this is what we should have been doing all our lives? If we don't, we can always call it off. There's no big investment involved. So let's tote up some kind of a Writer's Balance Sheet and take a look at what we have going for us, or agin' us, now that we're fifty or seventy or even ninety.

TO BEGIN WITH, THERE'S PREPARATION
Were we good planners-for-the-future way back in those hectic days when we were too busy to write? Did we keep a set of diaries or journals or files of writing information for future use? Do we have a well-organized sources system, a clear idea of how we are going to go about launching our new career? And are we prepared even at this late date to develop a "support system" that will enable us to write as efficiently as we once carried out our workday tasks in the past? If we are planning a family history, for example, do we have even a clue as to where there are branches of our fami-

ly tree or who the people are whose photographs are in that old family album? Or do we know who to call for help?

A convenient, suitably equipped writer's corner where we can work comfortably and efficiently is an asset if not an absolute necessity. Sure, we can write anywhere: on trains, planes, or buses—even underwater, if we had to—but we'll do better work if we have reasonably professional furnishings and equipment.

Our workshop, wherever it is, needs to be properly (but not overly) stocked with writing materials. We'll need pencils and pens and paper and carbons, but not in wholesale quantities. Let's be cautious at first. A filing system and a library of reference books are important start-up accessories. Above all, have lots of clear desk-top space.

Ensconced, privately if we wish or surrounded by activity, radio or television programs, and buzzing telephones, we can move on to

OUR WRITING OPTIONS

Not all of us (in fact a very few, relatively speaking) are going to settle down on Day One, at fifty or later, and begin writing a thousand-page novel, full-length autobiography, or history of the world. Nor are many of us intellectually equipped or knowledgeable enough to be in immediate demand as contributors to major newspapers or serious journals of opinion. Some of us may even prefer to write poetry for our own enjoyment or columns about dairy farming or berry picking for the agricultural press. Career opportunities for senior writers abound; it's a case of choosing the one—or ones—that interest us most and which we feel qualified to follow.

Here, in no special order, are just some of the options:

FICTION WRITING

Those who write from their imaginations instead of from facts are, for some strange reason, supposed to be the cream of the crop. A best-selling novelist is like a Metropolitan Opera star: A successful suspense writer can be translated into dozens of languages and live in a penthouse in the most expensive surroundings. There are, of course, thousands of lesser works of fiction published every year but the authors of these share some of the aura of the big-time artists and revel in the title of novelist.

To become a successful fiction writer one must almost have to be a born storyteller. The market is there for both novels and short stories but it is a tough one to crack. One advantage: A fiction writer may actually sit, snoozing in an armchair, and dream up a plot without the necessity of going searching for it. That's not very likely and hardly recommended, but a possibility. Short stories may present a less demanding challenge for a beginner. They're not easy to write but at least they don't take as much time in the writing.

NONFICTION

There is apparently an insatiable demand for books, magazine and newspaper articles, radio and television scripts, and motion picture scenarios about the world we live in and the people, animals, and plants that inhabit it. There is scarcely a subject—a personality, a place, a happening, an activity—about which something has not been written or is not in the process of being written. Yet the presses keep rolling, radio and television keep airing more and more informational programs. Within every Senior Citizen's memory box are stores of information waiting to be converted into tape or type.

There is always room for more books, more articles, or more films on any popular subject. Note, for example, the amazing proliferation of cookbooks. Preparing and eating food are international obsessions. In some cities entire bookstores are dedicated to information about cuisine. Church organizations publish cookbooks as fund raisers, governments and industries sponsor them as tourist or product promotions. What better legacy for a Senior Citizen to leave than a well-written cookbook preserving forever the original creations of his or her kitchen?

JOURNALISM

Here is the widest possible field for Senior writers; it includes hundreds and hundreds of publications with every possible editorial taste. Almost anyone interested in writing can, with some slight effort, find a niche here. With some training and initiative, it is possible to become a part-time correspondent or reporter for a

local paper; a columnist writing about a favorite hobby or craft;
an author of Op-Ed page commentaries; a book, theater, moving
picture, or dance reviewer, or art and restaurant critic; a sports-
writer covering local and regional games; a Senior Citizens' editor or columnist specializing in subjects of interest to mature
readers; a travel writer or business commentator.

There's something there for everybody.

OFF-BEAT MARKETS

Trade papers and company publications, commercial newsletters, church bulletins, association magazines, and annual reports—all hire free-lancers from time to time. The new and
booming enthusiasm for nostalgia will create new opportunities
for old-timers as special commemorative issues will be published
by hundreds of organizations. There are also continuing opportunities in advertising and public relations offices for free-lance
writers with experience in various professional or commercial
fields.

POETRY

Even here, diligent bards find book, magazine, and anthology
publishers willing to gamble on what used to be one of the most
popular and saleable of the literary arts. Readers lined up to buy
Byron's or Shelley's latest epics or collections from the pens of
Tennyson or Longfellow. Long lineups for our poems are not to be
counted on but, as Ralph Seager has demonstrated, a good poet
who self-publishes can earn a fair income.

LETTERS

Never should a Senior writer (or any other, for that matter) overlook the pleasure both given and gained through correspondence
by personal letter. The person who learns how to write a good letter and is fortunate enough to find an equally talented correspondent may be making an important contribution to the survival of
our civilized society. In no other writing form are the subtleties of
our daily lives so well preserved as in the person-to-person communications that every day cross continents and oceans to form
millions of contacts in our communicating world.

FRIENDS AND ENEMIES

Along our fresh, new trails into the world of literary creation we will encounter many individuals and institutions who will be our friends—or enemies. It is important that we learn to identify them, cultivate those who help us, and avoid those who don't.

THE GOOD GUYS

First, by all standards, is the editor who not only accepts our submission within reasonable time but goes to infinite pains to make sure that when it gets into print it will say in the most precise possible way what we meant it to say and will be clearly understood and enjoyed by the reader. Next, if we have a book manuscript or major magazine article to sell, it could be the literary agent who will use his or her knowledge and contacts to help market it. Through a professional agent we may win publication by a book or periodical publisher of whom we had never heard and who certainly had never heard of us. Unfortunately, benevolent editors and tireless literary agents are much in demand and are swamped with submissions from other writers who are looking for friends just as hard as we are.

Paradoxically, perhaps, counted among our good friends are scores of our competitors: successful writers who take time out from their writing hours to talk to us at seminars and workshops, teach at universities and colleges, and generally lend a helping hand to those of us who are attempting to invade their territory. We should watch for notices of their appearances locally and whenever possible attend their sessions and pay heed to their advice. One thing we should *not* do, in spite of Jim Kennedy's successful appeal to Saul Bellow, is to ask them to read, listen to, or critique our manuscripts. That would be imposing—not a friendly thing to do.

Instructors in established correspondence schools specializing in creative writing have been more than just teachers and have often become real mentors to many a struggling writer. Find one who can respond to your needs and give you a bit of individual attention and you'll be lucky. Check out the school or class first by contacting graduates, asking for proofs of success, and complain quickly if you think the course is a dud.

THE BAD GUYS

The writers' service industry is basically no different than those industries that serve other professions or businesses. There are good practitioners and bad ones. We can't always tell which is which at first glance. However, those to be wary of include: correspondence schools and agents who ask for "reading fees" before enrolling us as students or clients; editors who hold manuscripts longer than three months; subsidy or vanity publishers who accept our manuscripts with the proviso that we pay for the printing and publishing, promise a big marketing program, then let our books die, frequently still unbound, on the shelves; and friends, relatives, and neighbors who make our task more difficult by their lack of understanding.

Here we are, at last, at the bottom line. In the pages that follow are suggestions for tools that will help us—a reading list, directory of senior citizen writing schools, and other vital information. At the beginning of this book I said, "Welcome to the club." Now, 207 pages later, it's up to you to decide whether you want to join.

Bibliography

In addition to the books listed in this section, here are a few I've found especially good and want you to know about.

Our Language, by Simeon Potter (Penguin Books), was first published in 1910, and reprinted eight times before 1964 when I bought my copy. If we're going to write, we can never know too much about the words we use. Professor Potter tells it all.

For those planning Senior Citizen journalism, the answer is obvious: read the newspapers and magazines. Not just the big ones in New York, Boston, or Montreal, but the community papers—even neighborhood throwaways. All publications have a style, a manner of presenting the news, that you need to understand if you hope to ever write for them. Reading the newspapers is also a useful habit for writers in any field; that's where most of the plots come from, or the information to start you on nonfiction books or articles.

Speaking of words and newspapers, William Safire's weekly page about language in the *New York Times* Sunday Magazine is almost always amusing, informative, and instructive and puts you in a good mood for doing your own thing. And a copy of *The Elements of Style* is essential.

It's a good idea to check the supermarket or drugstore book stands carrying *Harlequin Romances* and look for the latest romance novel by Barbara Cartland to see what a spry octogenarian can still produce. Gwen Robins wrote a biography, *Barbara Cartland* (Doubleday, 1985), about this fascinating lady. A best-selling author for decades, Mrs. Cartland lists her interests as music, farming, aviation, decorating, nutrition, spiritualism, and public works—and manages to find time for them all. She gets up every day at 6 a.m., *reads* until noon, and works at her avocations till evening. Then she writes: a book or two—or four—a year.

And, finally, there's *Seeds*, the autobiography of the mother of Canadian tycoon Paul Pare, president of the giant conglomerate IAMSCO. The book's publication was announced by her son on Mother's Day, 1985. If you can't find *Seeds* listed in *Books in Print*, try writing to Paul Pare, President of IAMSCO, 4 Westmount Square, Westmount, Quebec, Canada. Mrs. Pare has written *her* first book well after fifty. She's ninety-seven.

Writing guides:

Bell, Norman. *Writers' Legal and Business Guide.* New York: Arco, 1984.

Bernstein, Theodore M. *Watch Your Language.* Channel Press, 1958.

Boggess, Louise. *How to Write Fillers & Short Features that Sell.* 2nd ed. New York: Harper and Row, 1981.

_____. *How to Write Short Stories That Sell.* Cincinnati: Writer's Digest Books, 1982.

Boles, Paul Darcy. *Storycrafting.* Cincinnati: Writer's Digest Books, 1984.

Golden, Stephen, and Kathleen Sky. *The Business of Being a Writer.* New York: Harper and Row, 1982.

Hanson, Nancy E. *How You Can Make $20,000 a Year Writing (No Matter Where You Live).* Cincinnati: Writer's Digest Books, 1980.

Hull, Raymond. *How to Write "How-To" Books and Articles.* Cincinnati: Writer's Digest Books, 1981.

Knott, Leonard. *Writing for the Joy of It.* Cincinnati: Writer's Digest Books, 1983.

Marcella, Frank. *Writing from Experience.* Englewood Cliffs, N.J.: Prentice-Hall, 1983.

Pitzer, Sara. *How to Write a Cookbook and Get It Published.* Cincinnati: Writer's Digest Books, 1984.

Polking, Kirk, and Rose Adkins. *Beginning Writer's Answer Book*, rev. ed. Cincinnati: Writer's Digest Books, 1984.

Polking, Kirk, and Leonard S. Meranus, eds. *Law and the Writer*, 3rd ed.: Cincinnati: Writer's Digest Books, 1984.

Rosenbaum, Jean, and Veryl Rosenbaum. *The Writer's Survival Guide.* Cincinnati: Writer's Digest Books, 1982.

Ruehlmann, William. *Stalking the Feature Story.* Cincinnati: Writer's Digest Books, 1978.

Shedd, Charlie. *If I Can Write, You Can Write.* Cincinnati: Writer's Digest Books, 1984.

Strunk, William, Jr., and E. B. White. *The Elements of Style*, 3rd ed. New York: Macmillan, 1979.

Tarshis, Barry. *How to Write Like a Pro: A Guide to Effective Nonfiction Writing.* New York: New American Library, 1982.

Teeters, Peggy. *How to Get Started in Writing.* Cincinnati: Writer's Digest Books, 1981.

Thomas, Frank P. *How to Write the Story of Your Life.* Cincinnati: Writer's Digest Books, 1984.

Zinsser, William K. *On Writing Well: An Informal Guide to Writing Nonfiction*, 2nd ed. New York: Harper and Row, 1980.

Zobel, Louise. *Travel Writer's Handbook.* Cincinnati: Writer's Digest Books, 1984.

Market Guides:

Books:

Deimling, Paula, ed. *1986 Writer's Market.* Cincinnati: Writer's Digest Books, 1985.

Fredette, Jean M., ed. *1985 Fiction Writer's Market.* Cincinnati: Writer's Digest Books, 1985.

Jerome, Judson, ed. *1986 Poet's Market.* Cincinnati: Writer's Digest Books, 1985.

Literary Market Place, 1985. New York: Bowker, 1985.

O'Gara, Elaine. *Travel Writer's Markets.* R. B. Shapiro, 1984.

Magazines:

The Writer
Writer's Digest

Organizations:

American Association of Retired Persons, 1909 K Street NW, Washington, DC 20049.

Director of National Programs, The Learning Exchange, P.O. Box 920, Evanston, IL 60204.

National Center for Educational Brokering, 211 Connecticut Avenue NW, Washington, DC 20036.

The National Community Education Clearinghouse Incorporated, 6011 Executive Boulevard, Rockville, MD 20852.

Scholarly Magazines:

Alternatives for Later Life and Learning, American Association of State Colleges and Universities, 1 Dupont Circle, Suite 700, Washington, DC 20036.

Interchange, The Learning Exchange, P.O. Box 920, Evanston, IL 60204.
Learning Times, College Board, Publication Orders, Box 2815, Princeton, NJ 08541.

Correspondence Schools:

Christian Writers' Guild, 260 Fern Lane, Hume, CA 93628.
Famous Writers School, 17 Riverside Avenue, Westport, CT 06880.
The Institute of Children's Literature, Redding Ridge, CT 06876.
National Writers Club, Suite 620, 1450 S. Gavana, Aurora, CO 80012.
Writer's Digest School, 9933 Alliance Road, Cincinnati, OH 45242.

Miscellaneous:

Dr. Charles Bolz, Louisiana Tech University, Box 7923, Ruston, LA 71272 (summer courses on computing).
Canadian National Institute for the Blind, 1929 Bayview Avenue, Toronto, Ontario, M4G 3E8, Canada.
Cheree Cargill, 457 Meadowhill Drive, Garland, TX 75043 (fanzines).
Eula Merry Harris, publisher, *The Roadrunner,* P.O. Box 25, Ocotillos, CA 92259 (information on amateur journalism).
Henry Lebensold, P. O. Box 25441, Tamarac, FL 33320 (experimental publication to which Seniors may contribute).
McGill University Center for Continuing Education, Redpath Library Building, 3461 McTavish Street, Montreal, P. Q. H3A 1Y1 Canada (special seminars for Seniors).
Stephen Sikora, % Reader's League, Box 6218, Albany, CA 94706 (copies of *Catalogue of Correspondence,* $1.00 SASE).
Recording for the Blind, Inc., 20 Reszel Road, Princeton, NJ 08540.

INDEX

Other Books of Interest

General Writing Books
    Beginning Writer's Answer Book, edited by Kirk Polking $14.95
    Getting the Words Right: How to Revise, Edit, and Rewrite, by Theodore A. Rees Cheney $13.95
    How to Become a Bestselling Author, by Stan Corwin, $14.95
    How to Get Started in Writing, by Peggy Teeters $10.95
    How to Write a Book Proposal, by Michael Larsen $9.95
    If I Can Write, You Can Write, by Charlie Shedd $12.95
    Knowing Where to Look: The Ultimate Guide to Research, by Lois Horowitz $16.95
    Law & the Writer, edited by Polking & Meranus (paper) $9.95
    The 29 Most Common Writing Mistakes & How to Avoid Them, by Judy Delton $9.95
    Writer's Block & How to Use It, by Victoria Nelson $12.95
    Writer's Encyclopedia, edited by Kirk Polking $19.95
    Writer's Market, $19.95
    Writer's Resource Guide, edited by Bernadine Clark $16.95
    Writing From the Inside Out, by Charlotte Edwards (paper) $9.95
Magazine/News Writing
    Complete Guide to Writing Nonfiction, edited by The American Society of Journalists & Authors $24.95
    How to Write & Sell the 8 Easiest Article Types, by Helene Schellenberg Barnhart $14.95
    Magazine Writing: The Inside Angle, by Art Spikol $12.95
Fiction Writing
    Fiction Is Folks: How to Create Unforgettable Characters, by Robert Newton Peck $11.95
    Fiction Writer's Market, edited by Jean Fredette $17.95
    Handbook of Short Story Writing, edited by Dickson and Smythe (paper) $6.95
    Storycrafting, by Paul Darcy Boles $14.95
    Writing Romance Fiction—For Love and Money, by Helene Schellenberg Barnhart $14.95
    Writing the Novel: From Plot to Print, by Lawrence Block $10.95
Special Interest Writing Books
    Complete Book of Scriptwriting, by J. Michael Straczynski $14.95
    The Craft of Lyric Writing, by Sheila Davis $16.95
    How to Write a Cookbook and Get It Published, by Sara Pitzer, $15.95
    How to Write a Play, by Raymond Hull $13.95
    How to Write & Sell (Your Sense of) Humor, by Gene Perret $12.95
    How to Write "How-To" Books and Articles, by Raymond Hull (paper) $8.95
    How to Write the Story of Your Life, by Frank P. Thomas $12.95
    On Being a Poet, by Judson Jerome $14.95
    Poet's Handbook, by Judson Jerome $11.95
    TV Scriptwriter's Handbook, by Alfred Brenner (paper) $9.95
    Travel Writer's Handbook, by Louise Zobel (paper) $8.95
    Writing for Children & Teenagers, by Lee Wyndham (paper) $9.95
    Writing for the Soaps, by Jean Rouverol $14.95
The Writing Business
    Complete Guide to Self-Publishing, by Tom & Marilyn Ross $19.95
    Complete Handbook for Freelance Writers, by Kay Cassill $14.95
    Freelance Jobs for Writers, edited by Kirk Polking (paper) $7.95
    How You Can Make $20,000 a Year Writing, by Nancy Edmonds Hanson (paper) $6.95

To order directly from the publisher, include $1.50 postage and handling for 1 book and 50¢ for each additional book. Allow 30 days for delivery.
    Writer's Digest Books, Dept. B, 9933 Alliance Rd., Cincinnati OH 45242
Prices subject to change without notice.